RALPH HUMPHREY

Giorgio Morandi's still-lifes at the World House Galleries are informed by an intuitive geometry without intellectual artifice, and an ascetic sensibility, painterly but without virtuoso flourish. He poses ordinary jugs and pots like holy family portraits, and paints them with a passion that is private, tender and unswerving. If Morandi's pictures are peasant-like in their simplicity, they are also aristocratic in the elegant, restrained and subtle ways in which quivering close colours are related and are suffused in a warm delicate light. These modest tranquil works are at once corporeal and immaterial, intimate and detached, so familiar that they have become abstract. Morandi succeeds in creating an immobility that evokes the eternal.

"WE HEAR IN IT AT ONCE
THE TENDERNESS TOWARD HUMAN DESIRE
THAT MODIFIES A TRUE FIRMNESS OF
MORAL JUDGMENT."

L.T. ON THE GREAT
GATSBY

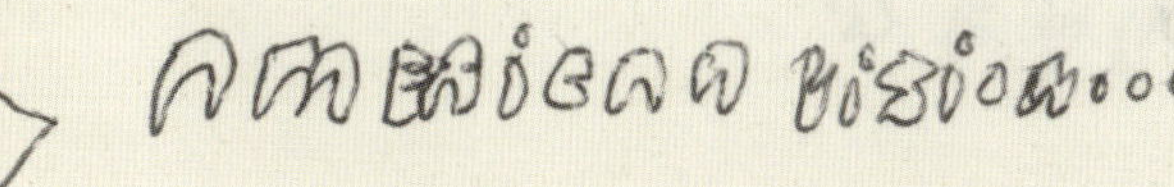

... IMPORTANT QUESTIONS
... WHERE THEY HAVE
BROUGHT AMERICA.
M.B.

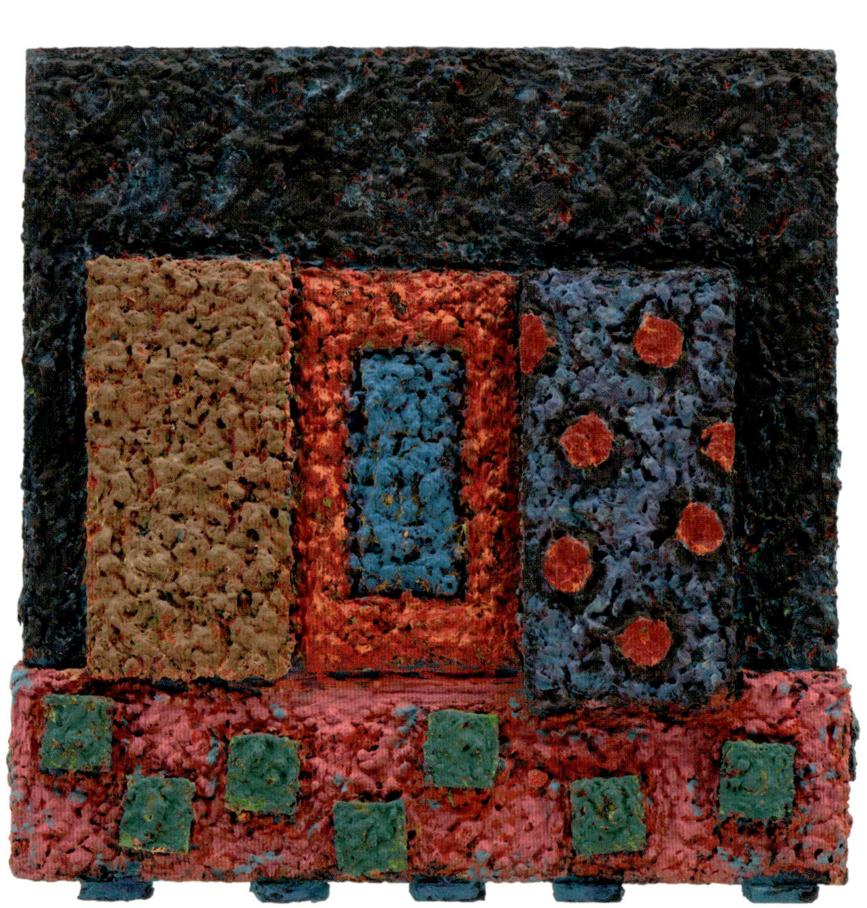

RALPH HUMPHREY

Gary Snyder Gallery, New York

The Space Around

Stephen Westfall

Artists find what they need to continue, or else they wither. One of the most meaningful exhibitions of any artist I have ever seen was Ralph Humphrey's 1976 show at the Daniel Weinberg Gallery in San Francisco. I was taking a year off before graduate school, collecting my thoughts, and sweating out LA "cool school" abstraction, which I was sugaring up to unpalatable levels. Too romantic for Minimalism and intimidated by its remorseless logic, I needed a kick. Humphrey's paintings from the mid-seventies provided it. My first impression was that they were as much sculpture as painting: oblique slabs like cut-open mattresses dipped in resonant, near-black violet, and blues that lifted up to a kind of daylight but that were still rooted to industrial shadows. Here were Bonnard's and Rothko's *ton sur ton* colors given an unprecedented materiality. Well, unprecedented to me.

I didn't as yet know Humphrey's earlier paintings: the gauzy monochromes, the luminous Frame Paintings, and the curved Shape Paintings. But the "wedge" paintings were both authentic and radical. They were authentic because of the way they resonated with the culture of painting and even sculpture. One could think of Bonnard and Rothko, but also of Braque's materiality, Cézanne's blues, and the space around Giacometti's figures. There was also precedent in the figural pre-Minimalism of Barnett Newman's "zips" and Ellsworth Kelly's body-scaled geometric semaphore. Yet Humphrey's paintings were also radical in the way they conflated an aggressive physicality with their resurgent lyricism. They didn't seem to be pictorial wholes so much as bitten-off chunks of architecture in the scale of human bodies.

The paintings are made with casein, a fast-drying milk-based paint that is more delicate than acrylic, but tougher than gouache, which it resembles in the matte brilliance of its color. The armatures were made of wood covered with a nappy-textured modeling paste, reminiscent of the stucco textures of the fake grottos that were built into late Renaissance and Baroque gardens. The fashion for the grotesque has never really left us, usually manifesting as an underground and often unconscious resistance to the rational forms of geometry. Humphrey was finding an essentialist means to fuse these Apollonian and Dionysian impulses. The volumes, the deep color, and even the diffused shadow embedded in the paintings' surfaces by the texture of the modeling-paste substrate all combined to assert physicality replete with interiority. Furthermore, it was a psychological interiority, as opposed to the "hollow" interiority that Michael Fried noted with both dread and exasperation in *Art and Objecthood* as a feature of Minimalist form-giving. There seems to be something inside Humphrey's forms, a secret that might be pried out. It might be histrionic to belabor Humphrey's homosexuality over this point, but it is no reach at all to suggest that being gay in the seventies would heighten one's own sense of interiority as a place of both resistance and refuge.

But the dimensionality of paintings such as *Conveyance #4* (1976–1977), *Untitled* (1975), and even the smaller *Untitled* (1975–1976), which is still three by four feet and deep as a large letterbox, pushes into real space. The psychology of Humphrey's paintings does not reside in a set of imagistic codes (although these emerge); it begins instead with its obdurate physicality. In a revealing passage from a 1982 interview with Amy Baker in *Artforum*, Humphrey describes the importance of Giacometti's influence in his developing conception of how a painting could enter a room:

RH: One of my earliest and biggest influences was the way Alberto Giacometti used surface to trap light so that his work doesn't just take up space, it makes you aware of space. I don't think his paintings are as resolved as his sculpture, but some are remarkable anyway because of what happens with line on the surface.

AB: *Isn't space more a sculptor's problem than a painter's?*

RH: *No. Painting alludes to frontal space. The whole issue of painting and sculpture in my work is more complex than either of the terms.*[1]

Humphrey is excepting his own painting from painting that "alludes to frontal space." His painting does that, too, of course, but it does more. Thus, his follow-up sentence, which serves as a key to understanding all the perceptual play set in motion by his paintings from the mid-seventies. A decade earlier, Frank Stella was also activating space in a sculptural way with his metallic striped polygons, and Barnett Newman's painting *The Wild* (1950) had abstracted Giacometti's sculptural figure into a painting sign more than a decade before that. But Humphrey's paintings seem to move with the viewer, offering other frontalities from shifting angles, unfolding over time. Stella's metallic striped paintings purposefully banished interiority and Newman was turning his zip into an animist totem. Nothing is wrong with either of their intentions; it's just that Humphrey was more concerned with a slower art, an experience of unfolding and accretion. What makes his work so affecting is how the paintings seem to reveal themselves in time, both singly and in relation to each other. Narrative, relational painting has always done this, but not radically abstract Minimal or Postminimal painting. And in narrative painting the space being read, or even *felt*, is inside the frame. Humphrey finds a new tension between interior and exterior space.

Thinking along these lines, it seems almost inevitable that his subsequent referential imagery would be the architectural subject of windows. The window emerges out of his own Frame Paintings and the apertures in his Shape Paintings, as well as from a renewed interest in European modernism. Mondrian's grid winks in and out of the window paintings, but it is the imagery and hot color of Matisse, Bonnard, and Vuillard that Humphrey is increasingly preoccupied with pumping into objecthood. In fact, transitional paintings, such as *For Norman* (1977) and *Flamingo* (1979), while clearly moving in the direction of window imagery, are still more or less abstract, like hairy, early Judds, coated with a sweet Pop irony of overlaid hues similar to the dye colors used in Trix cereal.

By 1980, the window image is firmly set in place and the impasto physicality of the paintings makes it hard to tell if we are looking in from the outside of each window or out from the inside. The wondrous *Christmas Story* (1979–1980) could give you reasons for thinking it's both. The light from the layered colors has a halo effect that feels like indoor incandescent light, whereas the little protruding nodules gridded across the surface feel like exterior Christmas lights; similarly, the Divisionist layers of color that emanate as an optical yellow-orange (there are greens, blues, and reds particalized in there, too), glowing beyond the turquoise mullions, could be a warm indoor light calling to the early evening.

Flamingo and *Christmas Story* also announce a new sense of Pop whimsy into what is fast becoming a referential imagery. *Thin Edge* (1981) and *Untitled* (1983–1984) are even more explicitly domestic windows with patterned curtains. In the schematic simplicity of their shapes and scale relations, the works recall illustrations of children's bedrooms from classic picture books such as *Goodnight, Moon*, and *Harold and the Purple Crayon.* For many of us, our childhood bedroom window is the beginning of our imaginative threshold. Humphrey takes this image and fuses it with the icon of Modernist painting, the architectonic grid. He uses wood slats to build the window forms off the surface of the canvas before applying the textured modeling paste. Every area that would correspond to our ideas of where the panes would go is recessed a bit from the ridges and edges of these wooden slats. The paintings move back toward abstraction for a spell in 1984, as the "window" is superimposed onto wood panels with curved corners, similar to the paintings of the early seventies.

Philip Guston's late figurative work inspired the cartoon simplicity of Humphrey's forms (there's mention of Guston in the Baker interview); their objecthood comes from Judd and Johns (interestingly, Johns is making Guston-influenced imagery about this time); and the tactility, color, and pattern are all from the School of Paris. And this encyclopedic painterly conversation produces wholly recognizable Ralph Humphreys. But Humphrey himself is shaking this consistency a bit toward the end of his life. His late interior still lifes, such as *Untitled* (1985–1987), are still framed by a window, but they are shying a bit into diagonal perspectives, like the *Nabis* paintings that were so influenced by Japanese *ukiyo-e* prints. There is a new animation in these paintings, as though the breeze lifting the curtains in *Thin Edge* could finally bend the illusionistic space within the picture. I don't see these paintings as a renunciation of abstraction, as there was always a lyrical voice in even his most imposingly abstract works. And yet, at the end, we're finally allowed to look through the window and see what's inside: a table with patterned cloth and a leafy plant, the angle of the table leading to a shadowed beyond. *Bonjour, Messieurs Vuillard et Matisse*. *Bonjour, Monsieur Mort*. Humphrey died, as most of us do, too young. I would have liked to explore that room a little further.

Humphrey's work provides even greater inspiration, affirmation, and solace for me today than it did that afternoon in San Francisco many years ago. This is because I have been nurtured all along by the conversation with the phenomenology and history of form that is painting culture, and in Humphrey I see a kindred spirit, someone to aspire to, and someone I want to continue the conversation with. Humphrey understood that abstraction doesn't have to be purged of memory, that it, in fact, probably can't. And he also saw that painting is a part of architecture, that it establishes a kind of social theater in a room. Or, put it this way: Place a few paintings in a room and they compel. Put too many in and they're hard to see, or *feel*, even as they turn the room into a salon. Few artists have demonstrated painting's dynamic relationship to the space around it as beautifully and decisively.

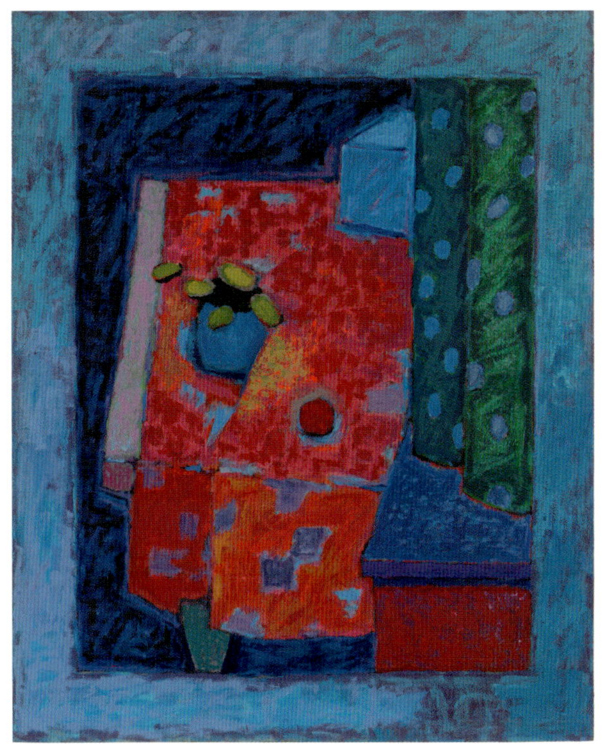

Untitled, 1985–1987

1. Amy Baker, "Painterly Edge: A Conversation with Ralph Humphrey," *Artforum* 20, no. 8 (1982): 38–39.

Untitled, 1973

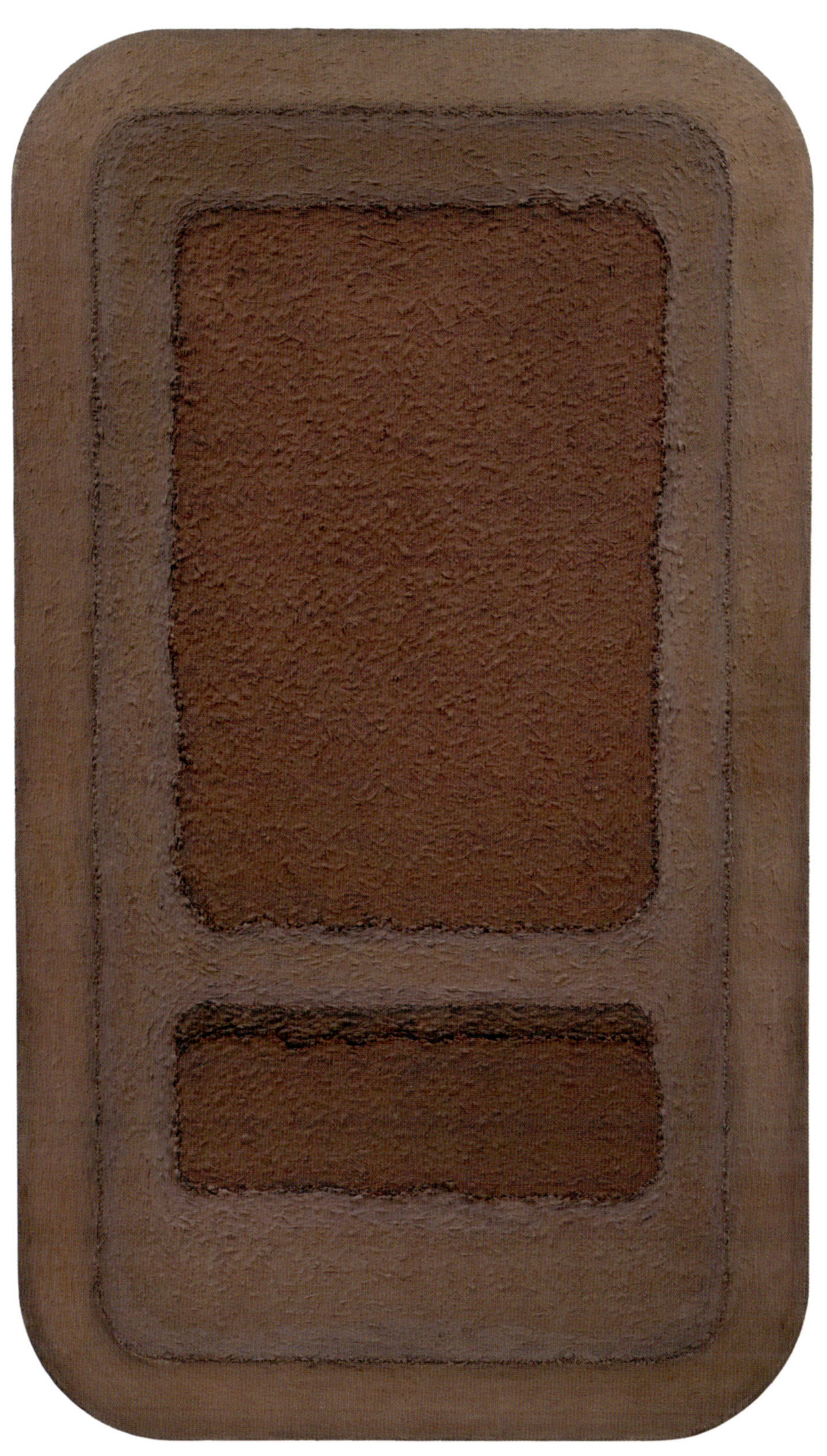

 Untitled, 1975

Conveyance #4, 1976–1977

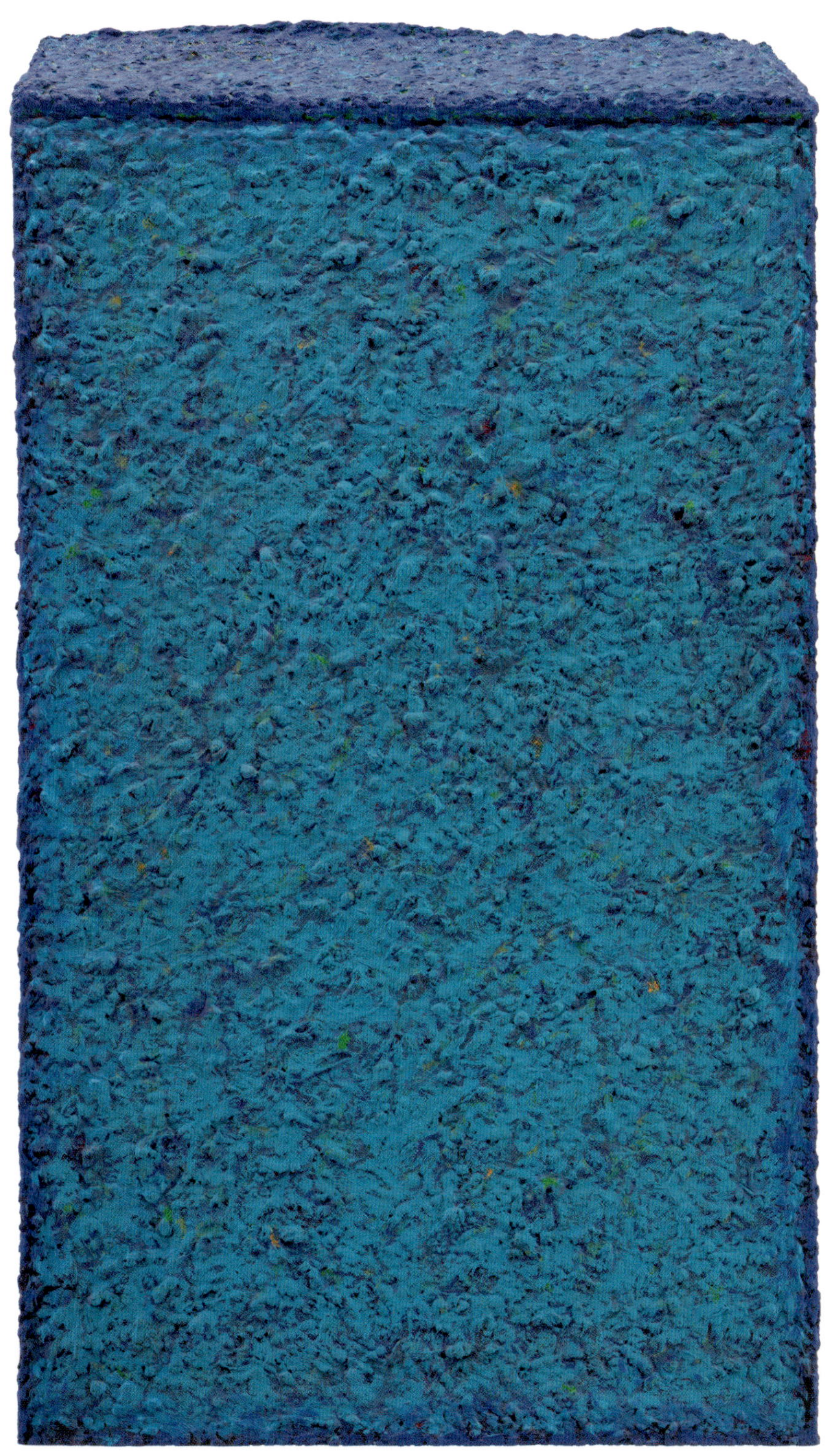

For Norman, 1977

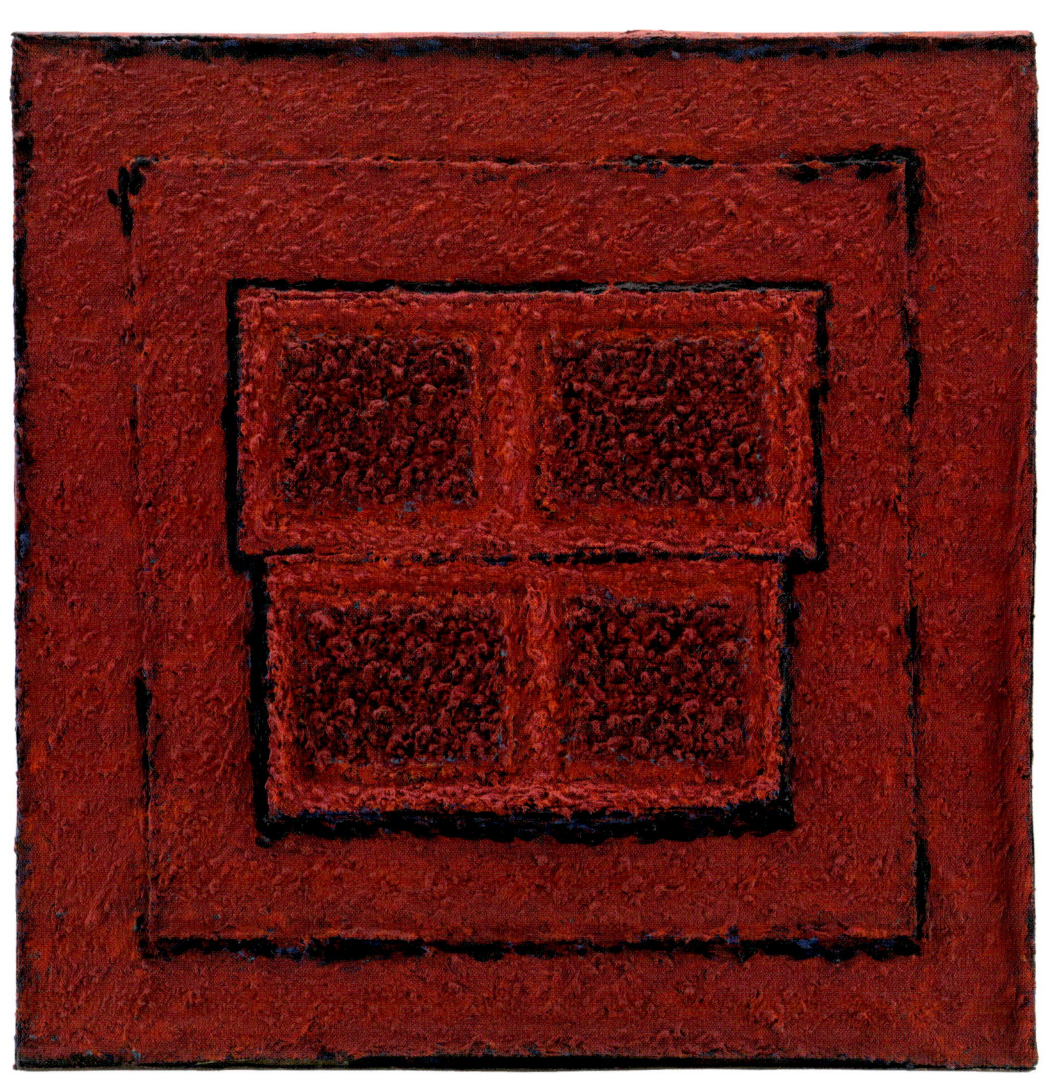

16 **Untitled**, 1977

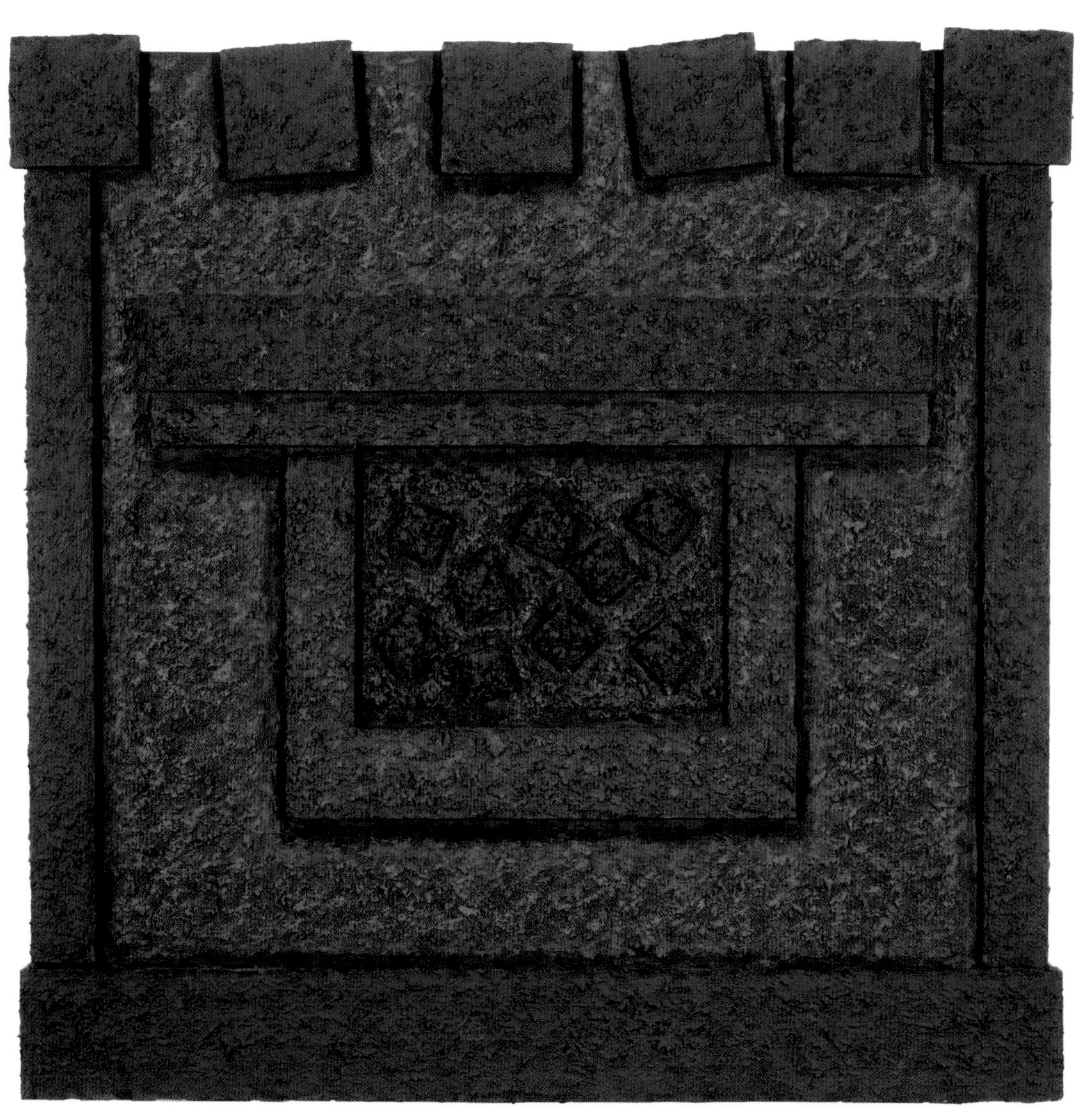

Flamingo, 1979

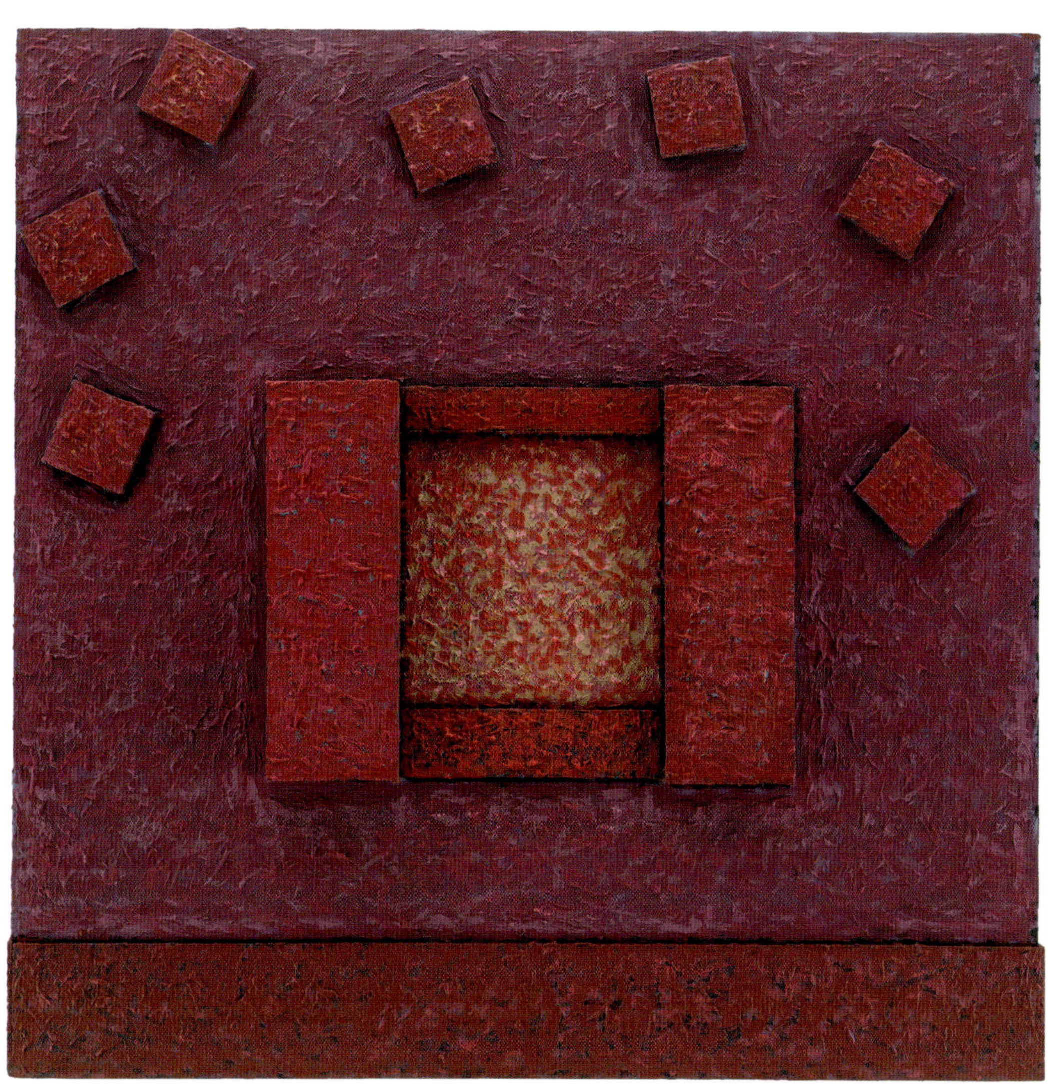

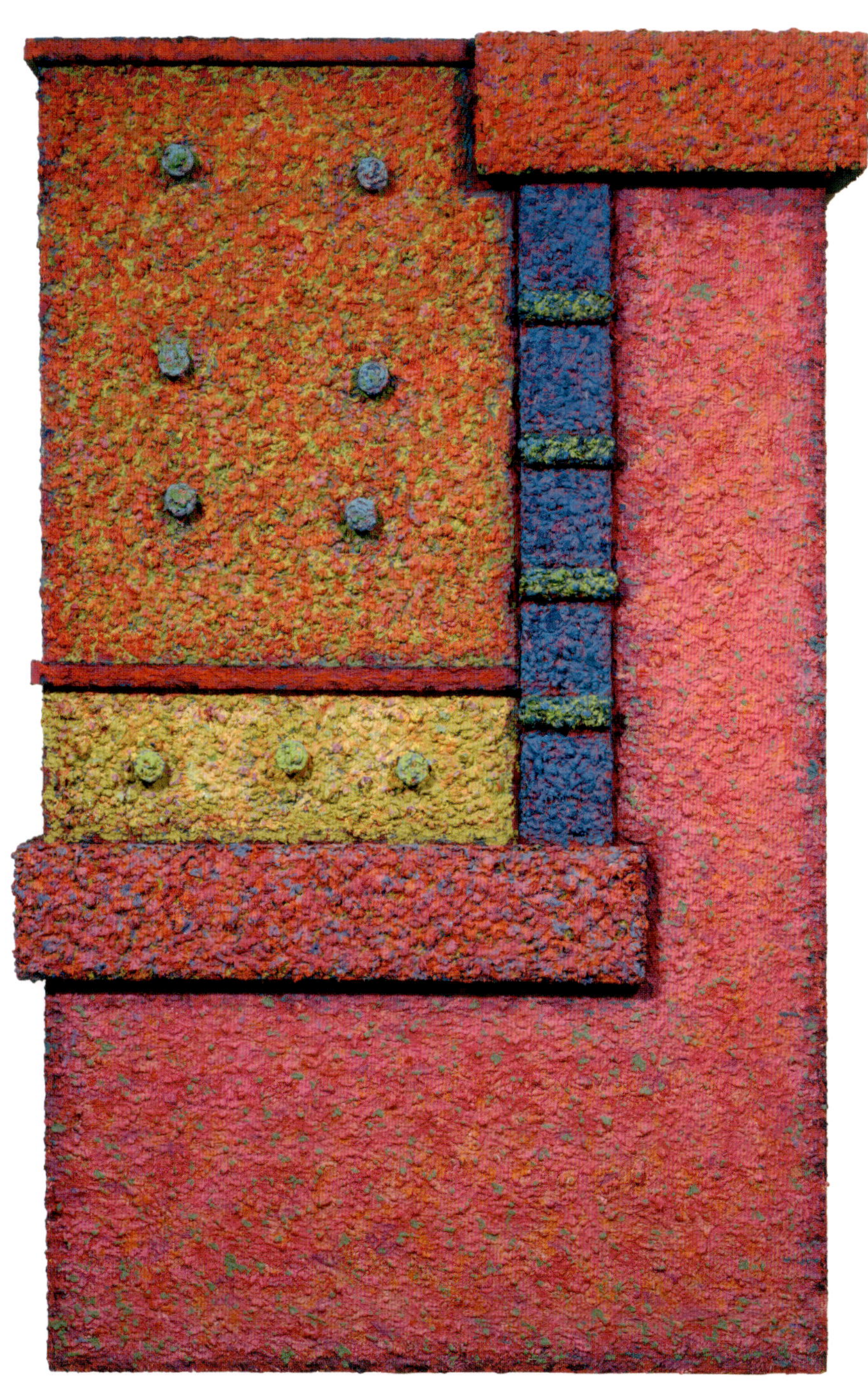

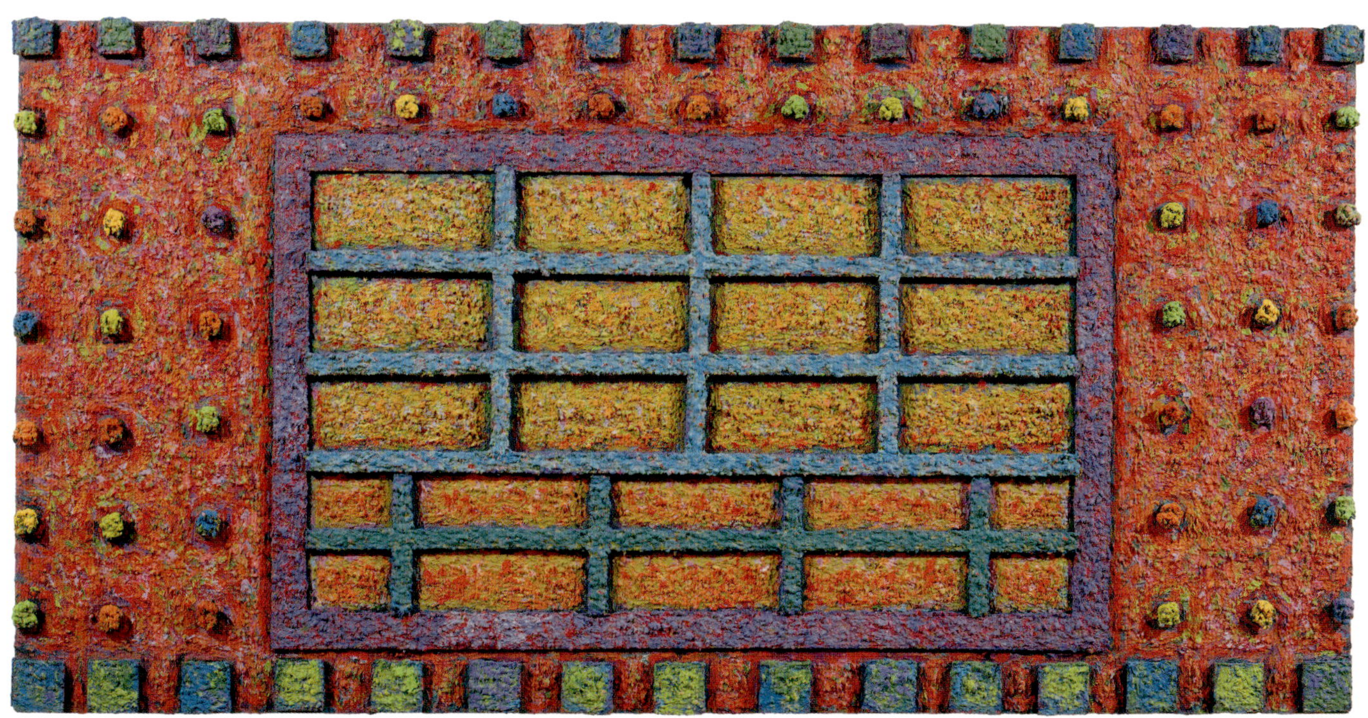

Thin Edge, 1981

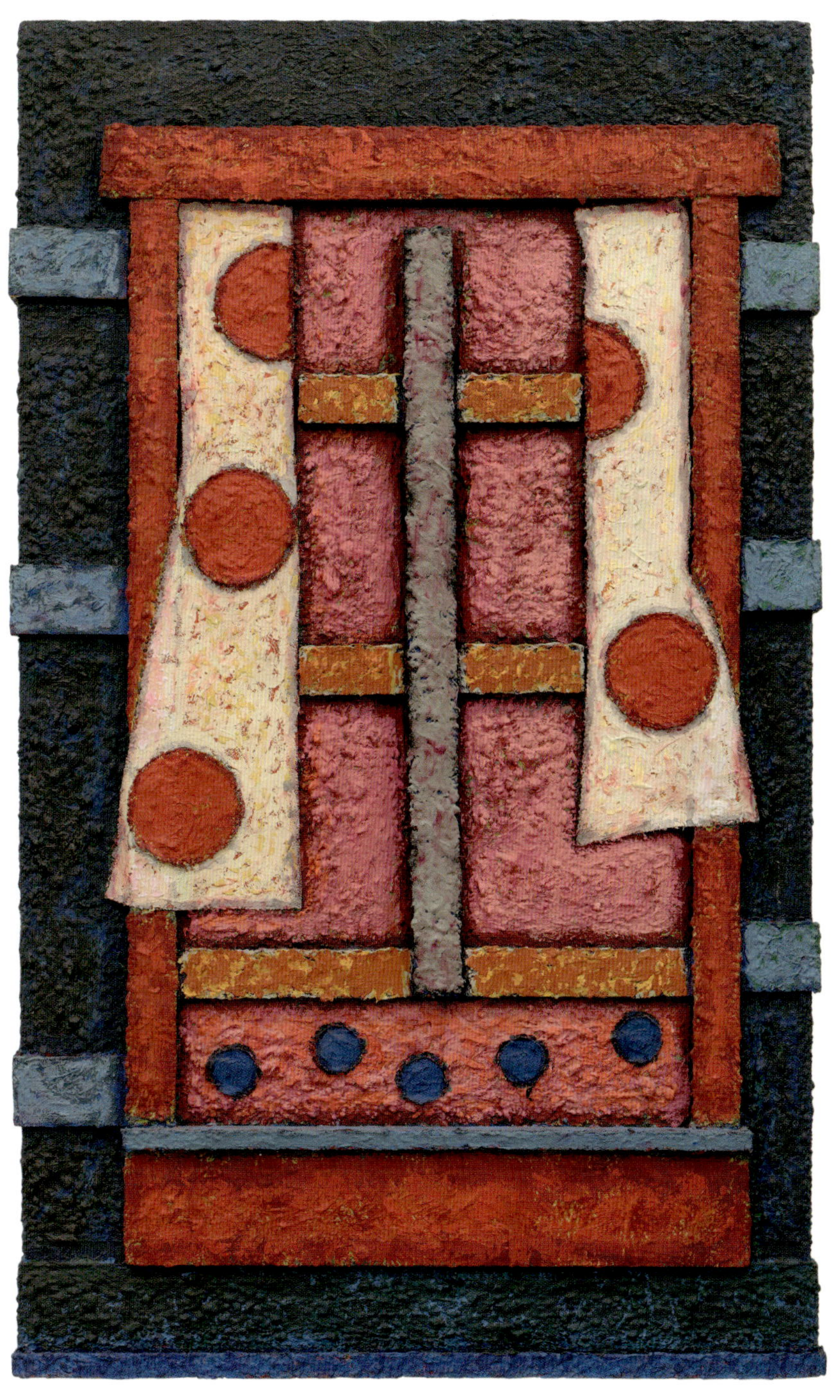

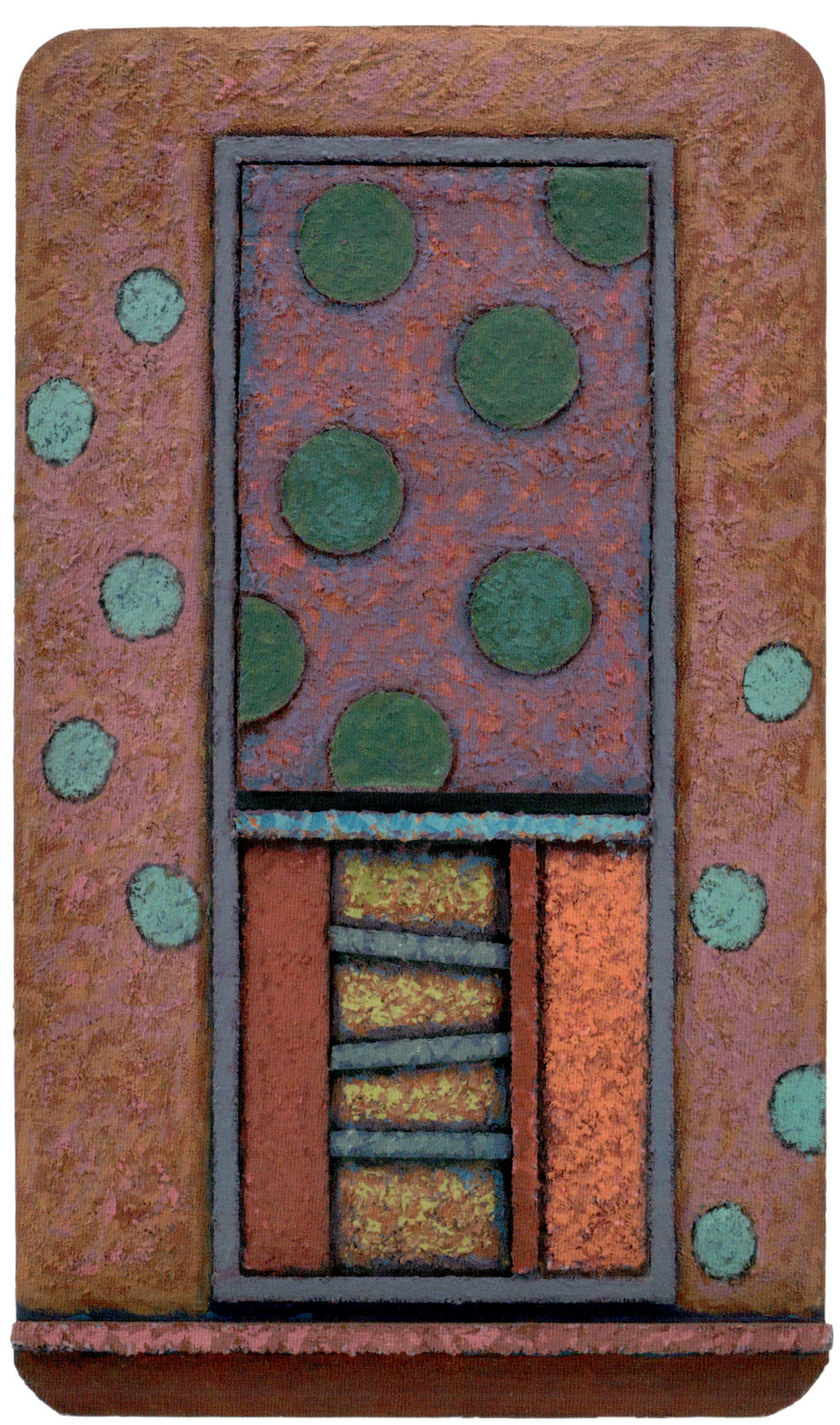

Untitled, 1983–1984

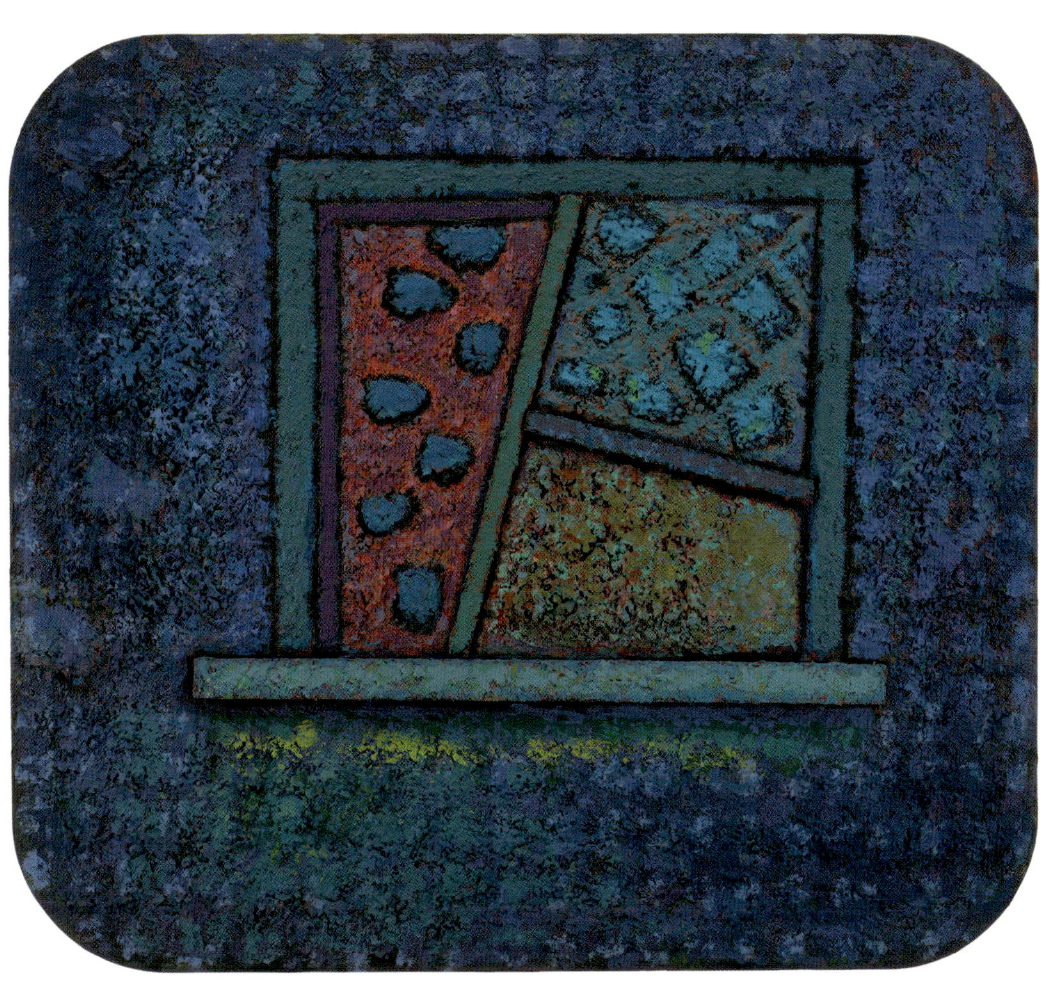

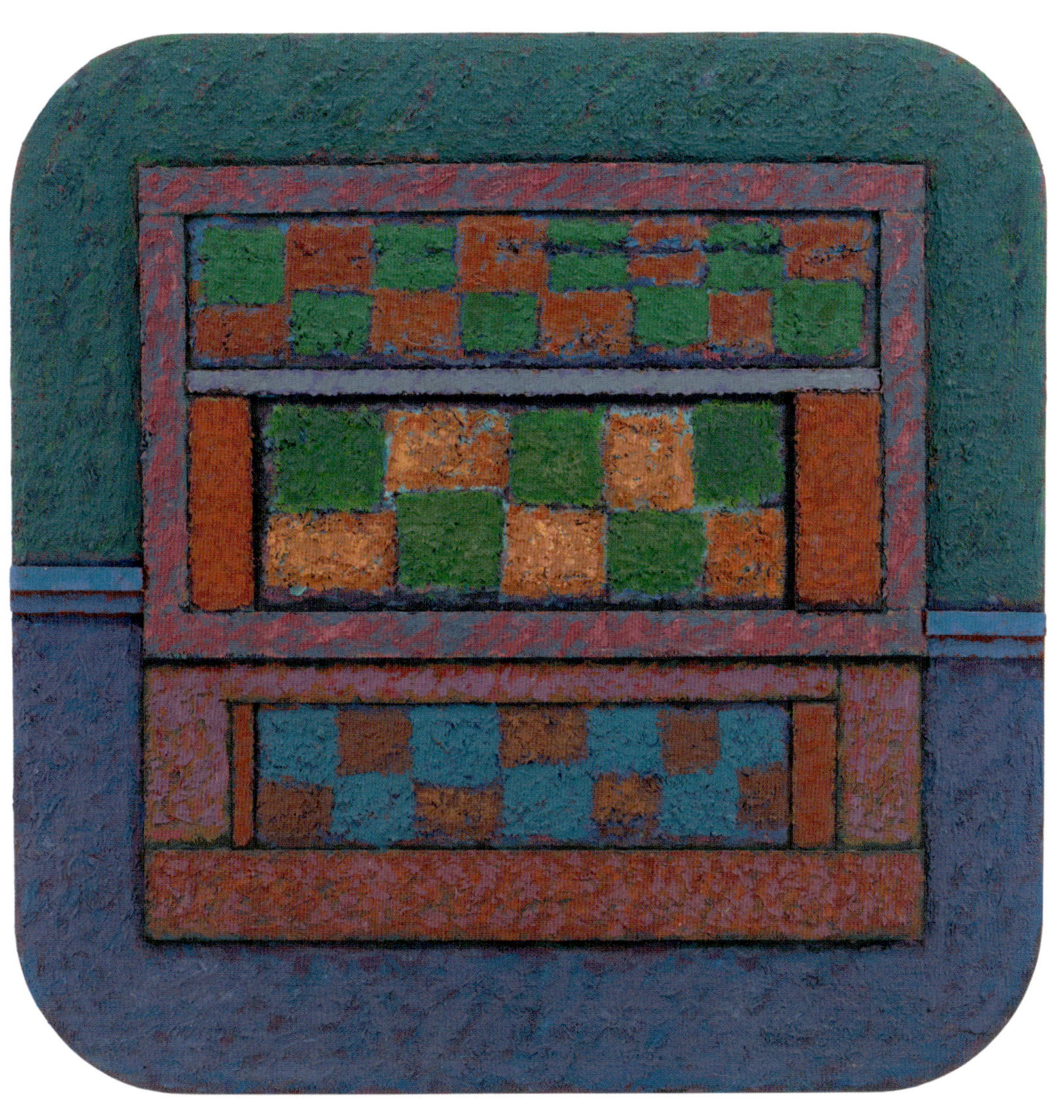

Mountain, 1983–1984

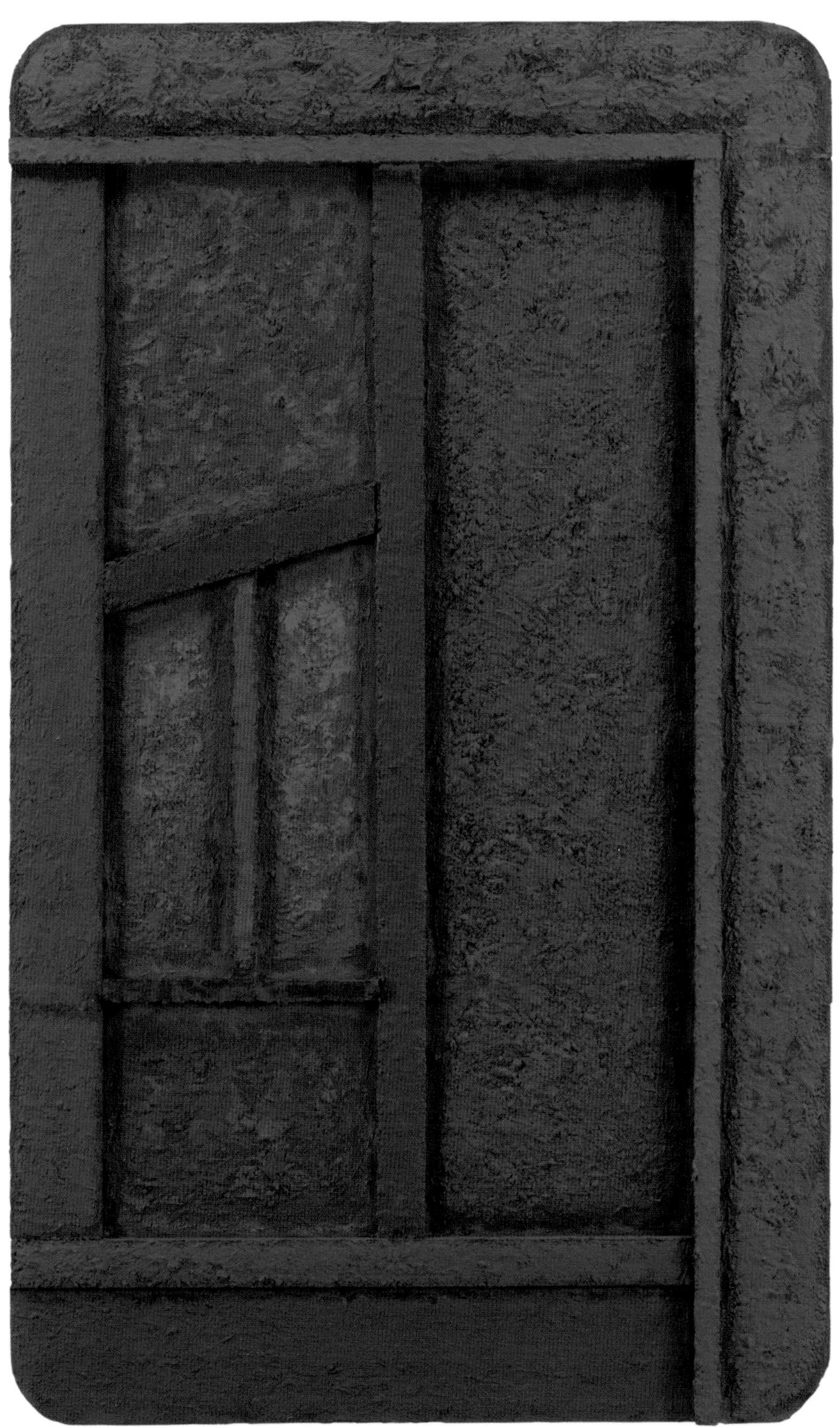

Forest, 1984

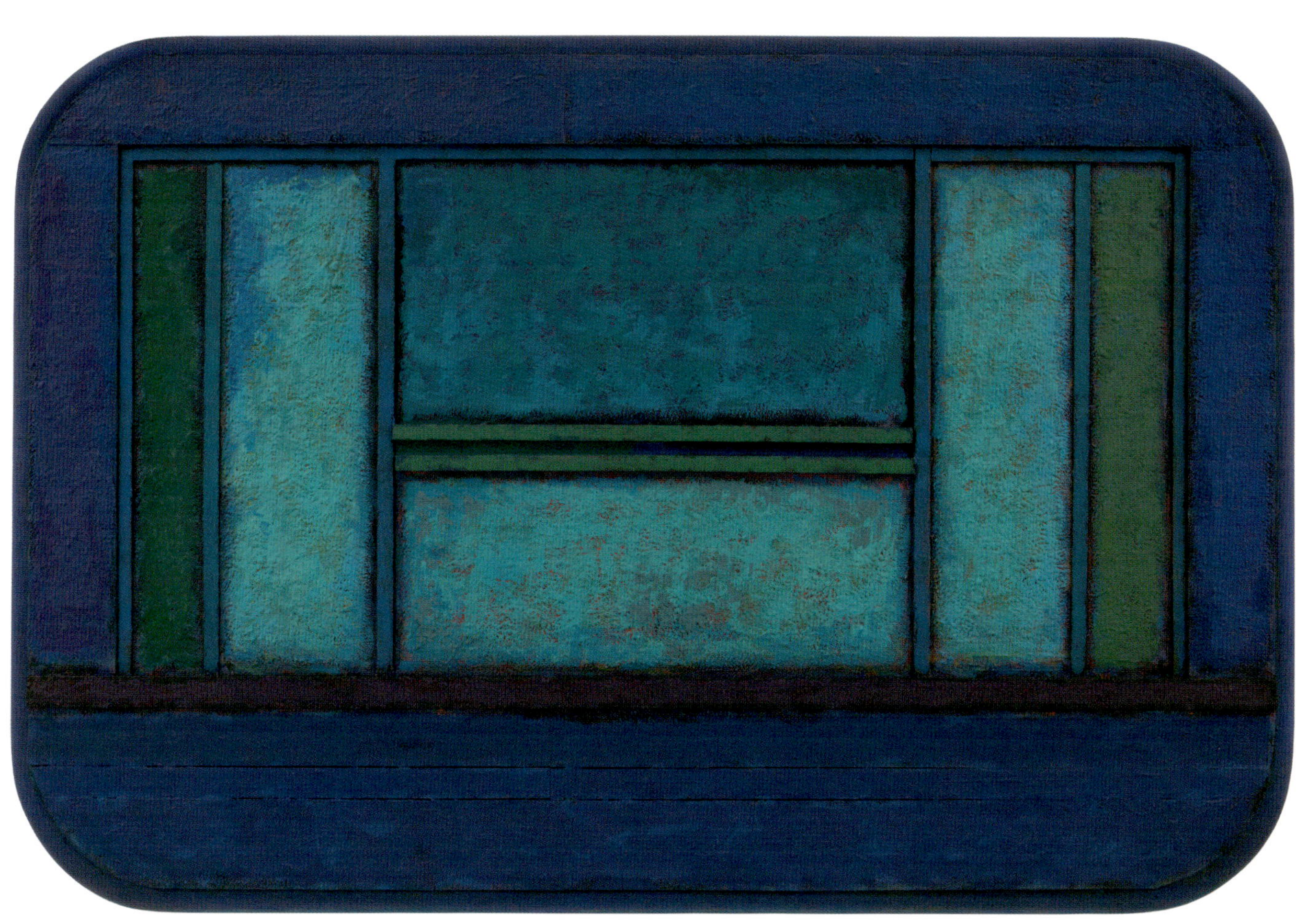

Desert, 1984

Border, 1984

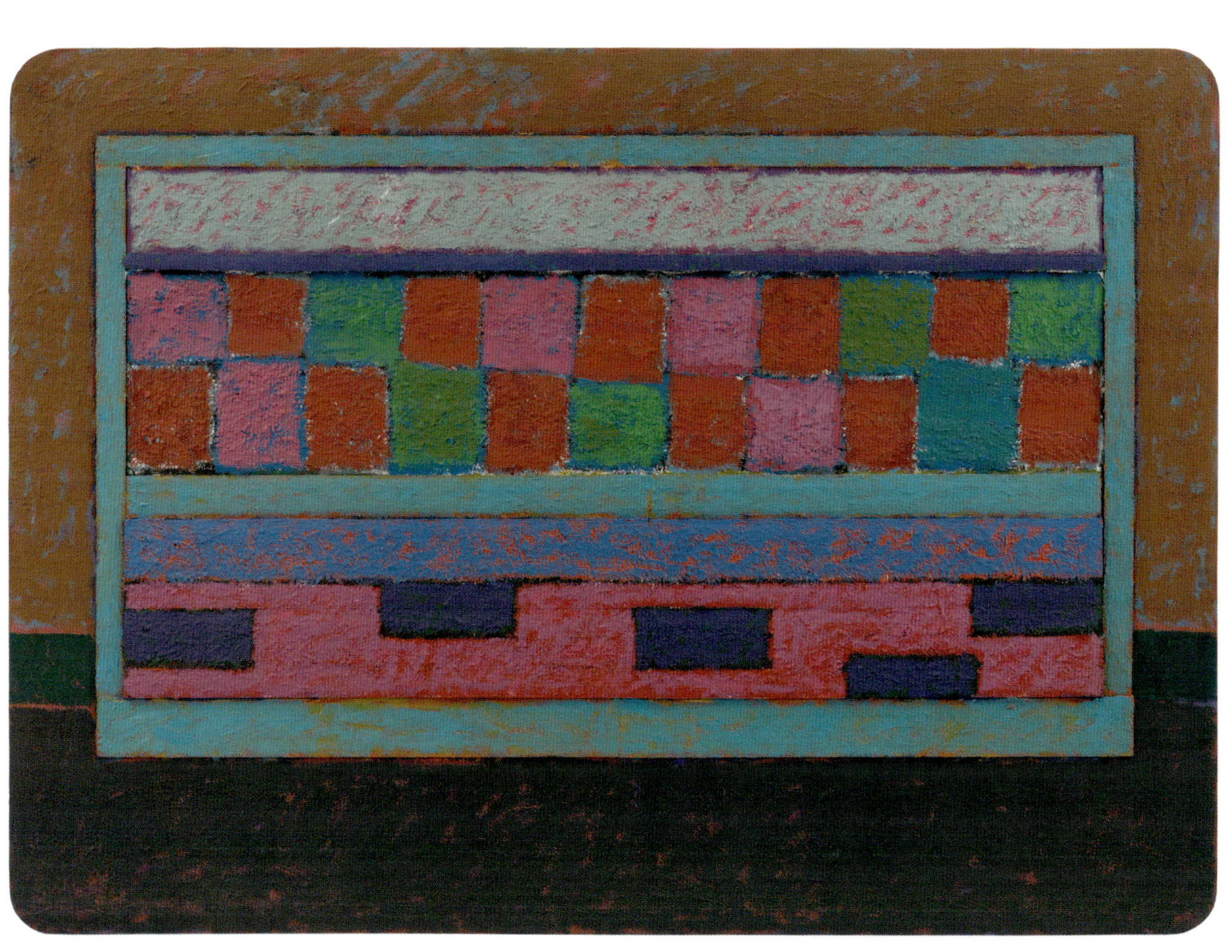

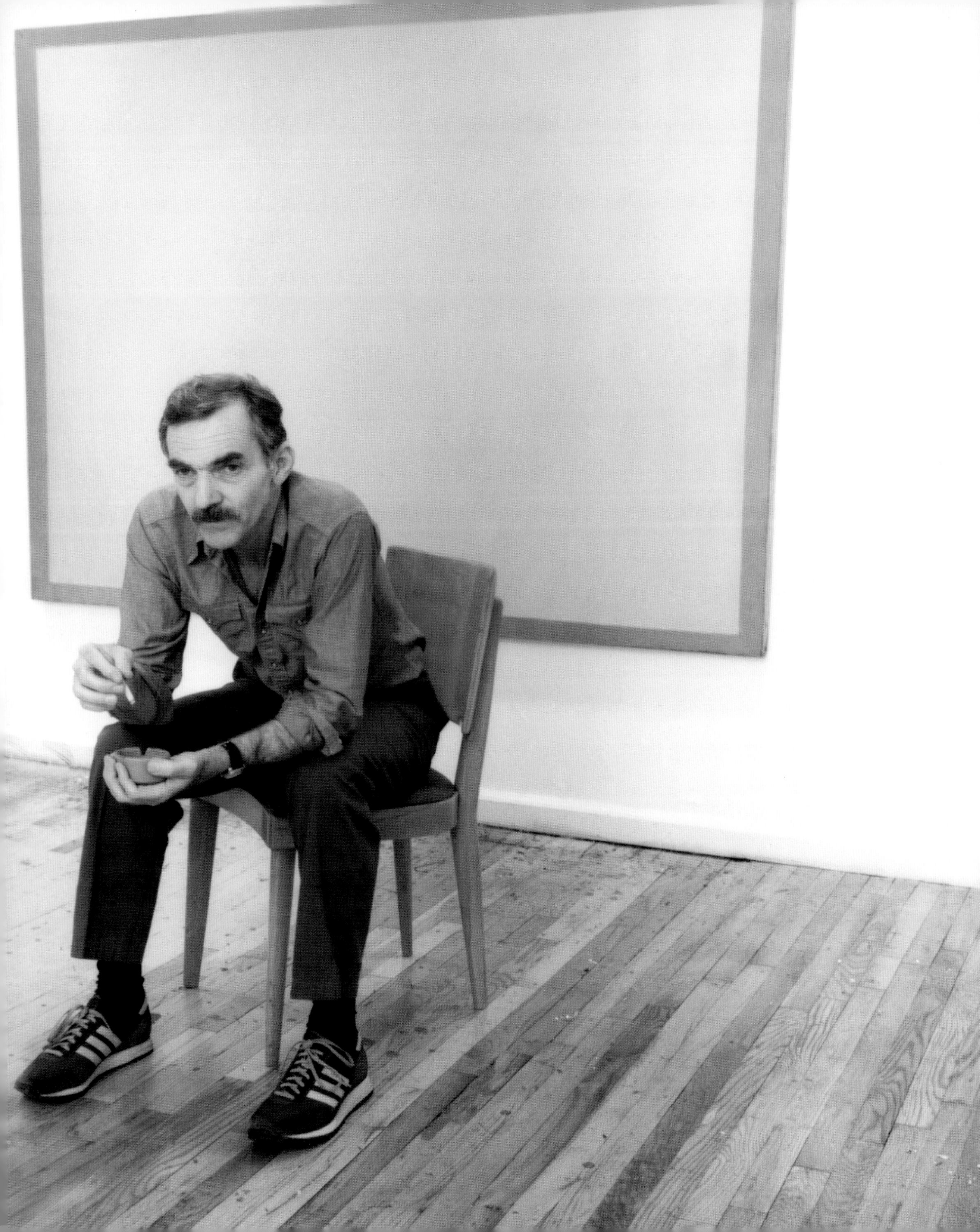

Inside Outsider

David Pagel

If I didn't know any better, I'd say that Ralph Humphrey was a California painter.

A sensitive freethinker, his deliciously inventive blends of painting and sculpture, abstraction and representation, meaning and matter, as well as sensual pleasure and cognitive dissonance, formal rigor and funny business, flat-out nuttiness and bare-naked love, align him with an impressive list of go-it-alone eccentrics who were either born in Southern California or have been coming here since the sixties to do their variously original things. Generally unencumbered by such institutional support structures as museums, markets, and the slippery web of expectations that accompany, often deleteriously, careers, reputations, and lives in the arts, such artists as Lee Mullican, Ken Price, Charles Garabedian, and Richard Allen Morris, as well as Jim Isermann, Brian Calvin, and Michael Reafsnyder, have found fertile ground in California, where their out-of-step, out-of-school, out-of-this-world works reflect the do-as-I-please ethos that often flourishes away from the spotlight, not exactly beneath the radar or off the beaten path, but more than a little off-center—deliberately off-kilter, precisely out-of-whack, inescapably idiosyncratic, even borderline preposterous.

The ham-fisted simplicity, blunt dumbness, and this-is-it obviousness that take potent shape in their materially insistent works, mask a kind of sophistication that is, well, sophisticated: complex and nuanced and committed to getting past the mere appearance of sophistication and its cohorts—elegance and refinement. Such signs of high tastefulness are not necessarily hollow, pretentious, or cliquey, but they come far too close to the sort of mannered privilege and assumed entitlement that art from California typically works against in its humble celebration of pedestrian pleasures, little epiphanies, and down-to-earth transcendence. That is exactly what Humphrey's works do, every day of the week, every time you lay eyes on them.

Weird beauty is their modus operandi. It goes hand-in-glove with such workmanlike virtues as do-it-yourself ingenuity and finish-the-job perseverance, neither of which gets fetishized as preciously collectible ends-in-themselves or condescendingly valorized as exotic signs of simpleminded integrity (otherwise known as folksy naivety). Rather than playing along with the fantasy that art elevates the drudgery of everyday life by puffing it up into something special that must be visited in a museum, Humphrey's casually masterful and disarmingly flat-footed works, along with their Left Coast counterparts, prefer the quotidian humility and no-nonsense pragmatism of the workaday world, which is replete with its own mysteries and pitfalls, dramas and dreams, puzzles and pleasures.

A sense of come-one, come-all accessibility suffuses Humphrey's user-friendly art, which welcomes—and generously reciprocates—the unpredictable give-and-take of real conversations. The meandering twists and turns of these back-and-forth exchanges complicate, but do not block, see-for-yourself discoveries, which are all the sweeter for being hard won. More like conversations with yourself than arguments with others, the dialogues Humphrey's curiously contemplative works generate are interior, silent, and self-reflective—as passionately charged as any intense disagreement with anyone else, but more befuddling, doubt-riddled, and laced with uncertainty than are most conflicts with others. Ambiguity and ambivalence, which almost always disappear from two-party debates—and don't even enter the arena of public discussions, because they might hint at weakness—have more room to maneuver in our intimate endeavors to hash things out with ourselves, mulling things over, weighing our options, pondering the possibilities, envisioning consequences, and speculating about next steps as we strive and stumble to find some sort of workable balance between what we feel in our guts and what our heads tell us. These are the kinds of conversations Humphrey's paintings engender as they, like great teachers, do not merely *tell* us how things are, but *show* us how they work, concretely and vividly, and as if nothing in the world were more important than our understanding.

In a sense, all works of art are custom-made. But Humphrey's thickly encrusted relief pictures are uncannily customized—in an inside-out, yet profoundly effective manner. Not a whiff of made-to-order pickiness or fussy, half-decaf/half-skim/hold-the-cream specialness drifts into the Everyman anonymity of his slow-brewed works, which, in making a virtue of clichéd subjects and generic formats, still somehow manage to seem as if they were made for you, and you alone—in this very moment, right here and right now. Part of that has to do with the fact that Humphrey's paintings do not begin in the aftermath of implied events, which, by the simple fact that they precede our interaction with his paintings, are endowed with more importance than anything that might happen in the present. Another part of their power resides in the simplicity of the things they depict—windows, walls, curtains, and boxes—and the lumpen luxury of Humphrey's paint-handling, which is anything but precious yet never slapdash, cavalier, or careless. The collision between these two elements—the *what* and the *how*—compels us to stop scanning our surroundings swiftly, in a rush to glean what's significant to our narrow purposes, and, instead, to dive into the details, to embrace their strangeness, and to get lost wondering *why*. This brings us to the third, and most important, aspect that animates and enlivens Humphrey's potent paintings: their face-to-face, one-on-one, can't-be-duplicated, can't-be-repeated intimacy. With more ease than drama, and no fanfare whatsoever, there comes a time when the painting you have been staring at suddenly seems not to have been made *for* you, as much as *with* you, in a participatory sense of shared responsibility.

The sensuous physicality of every last nook and cranny forms the heart and soul of Humphrey's oddly serene works, which are far more concerned to make something happen in the present than to record something that happened in the past. The same goes for trying to signify anything that is supposed to be significant: Humphrey could not care less about such abstract meaning-making—not because it's futile, but because that's just not the way his painstaking paintings work as they strive to make a place for the possibilities of playfulness in a world governed by ruthless efficiency and administered by instantly delivered messages. In his terrifically out-of-sync paintings, each multilayered patch of pigment, casein, and canvas becomes a world unto itself. As you move around its craggy contours, the colors shift subtly, shadows lengthen and disappear, depending on the intensity and angle of the ambient light, and time does not stand still so much as every moment gets so jam-packed with so much to see that it seems to last a lot longer than usual. Such experiences eventually end, but they live on in our memories, where they can be revisited, over and over again. Even so, there's nothing as rejuvenating as seeing a painting by Humphrey in the flesh, its freshness always better than even the best recollections.

In front of Humphrey's densely built-up panels, which are weighty and should seem heavy but still manage to float free of such fact-focused literalism, we do not wonder about ponderous philosophical issues, such as *"What does it all mean?"* as much as we ask ourselves *"Why don't we take notice, more often, of the mind-blowing beauty of what's right in front of our eyes?"* Such little things as the ways various dabs of paint interact suddenly matter more than usual, perhaps the way a speck of sexy red hums with mysteriously soothing intensity alongside a juicy rainbow of purples, burgundies, and blues—from the resplendent end of the spectrum. At once incidental and extraordinary, such experiences may not make sense to our rational selves.

But we know, once we experience them, that it would be irrational to dismiss them. After seeing a painting by Humphrey, rationality is not what it was. Neither are we.

In any case, the logic of monologues, the certitude of rants, and the structural antagonism of argumentation, scholarly and otherwise, are dispensed with by Humphrey's intimate pictures of ordinary things, all of which invite us to have conversations with ourselves. How these conversations play out is not prescribed by the paintings. All that matters is that we have them. At a time when public discussion is increasingly overrun by one-dimensional diatribes, and when what passes for analysis is thumbs-up approval or thumbs-down rejection, the sense of open-ended possibility that takes shape in Humphrey's paintings takes on a political dimension. As powerful counterexamples to the status quo—or as islands of quiet in a sea of screaming messages and eye-grabbing cacophony—his stubborn holdouts for something different extricate themselves from business as usual in order to make room for such things as the freedom to make up one's own mind, and then to change it, all the while holding incompatible, even contradictory, ideas in one's head. That may make you an unlikely candidate for public office, but it's the only honest way to live with yourself.

The main difference between Humphrey and his California counterparts is that his artistic identity was forged at a time and place that was, for all intents and purposes, the center of the universe, at least in terms of abstract painting. Whatever Los Angeles was when Mullican (b. 1919, Chickasha, Oklahoma), Garabedian (b. 1933, Detroit), Morris (b. 1933, Long Beach, California), and Price (b. 1935, Los Angeles) came into their own as artists, it was not the center of art's universe. In Los Angeles, these independent-minded mavericks found the freedom to do what they wanted. They also found that freedom and anonymity went together, as the general public's basic disregard for what they were up to left them free to do what they wanted and needed. By the time Isermann (b. 1955, Kenosha, Wisconsin), Calvin (b. 1969, Visalia, California), and Reafsnyder (b. 1969, Orange, California) emerged in the 1990s, Los Angeles was no longer a backwater. Considered to be a major art center in a newly global art world, its high-profile reputation came with some of the same constraints that Humphrey had struggled against throughout his career, namely, having one's art turned into an empty emblem of one's branded identity, and the even greater difficulty of knowing the difference between what it is that you do as an artist and the myths that grow up around art whenever enough people pay attention. It's no accident that Isermann lives in Palm Springs, Calvin in Ventura, and Reafsnyder in the suburbs of Orange County. Back in 1970, Price saw the writing on the wall and got out of Los Angeles, taking up residence in Taos, New Mexico. Morris never even moved to Los Angeles, staying in San Diego after wrapping up a stint in the military.

When Humphrey moved to New York from his childhood home of Youngstown, Ohio, in 1956, he was immediately in the thick of things, confronting, on a daily basis, the legacy of Abstract Expressionism, the emergence of Pop and Minimalism, and, most maddeningly, the transformation of an art scene—made up of passionate participants—into an art world, which was more like a spectator sport and included a level of investment-driven speculation that was new to Manhattan. As time went on, Humphrey did not have the luxury of getting out of town. But he never settled into a signature style that could be easily marketed. Instead, his career is marked by the kinds of shifts that look incoherent to viewers in search of neatly packaged series yet make profound sense to people who pay attention to the experiences that mattered to Humphrey. His stay-at-home, go-it-alone sensibility resonates on both coasts, drawing deep allegiance from viewers who have no time for naivety but will go to great lengths to get a glimpse of real innocence.

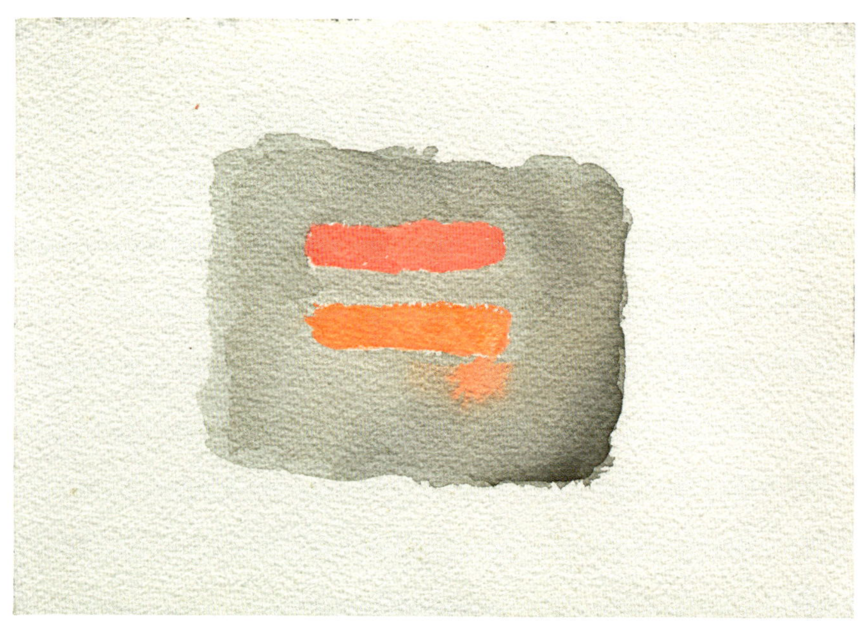

Untitled, 1973

Untitled, 1976

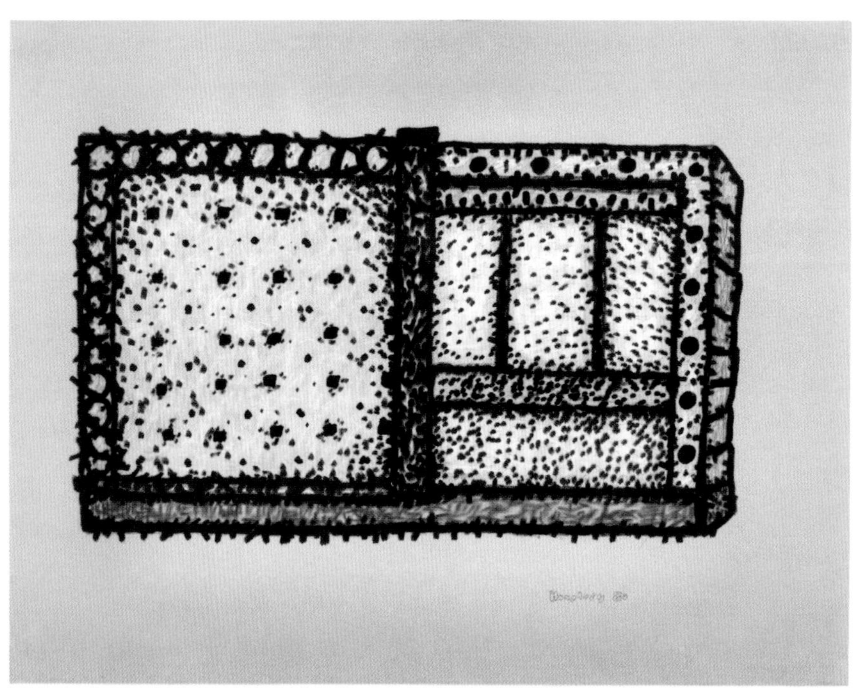

 Untitled, 1980

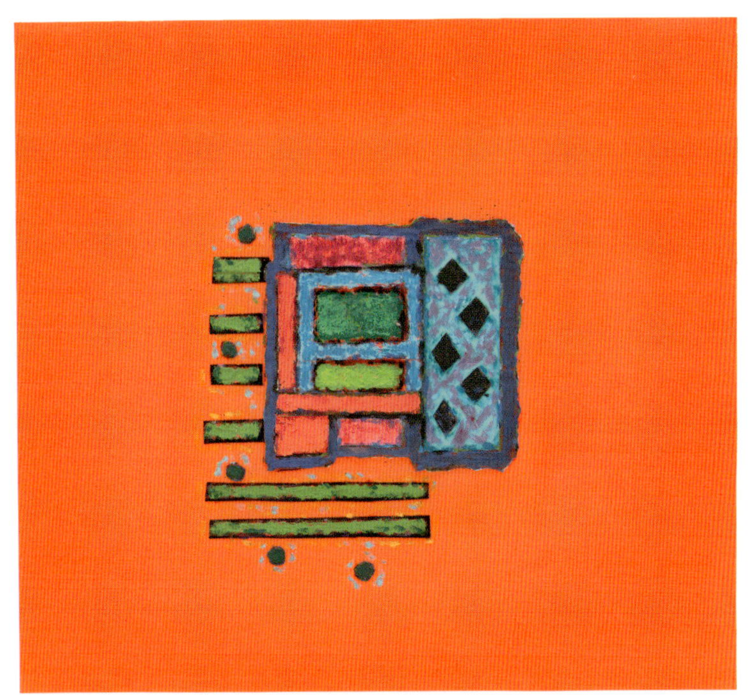

Untitled, c. 1979–1980

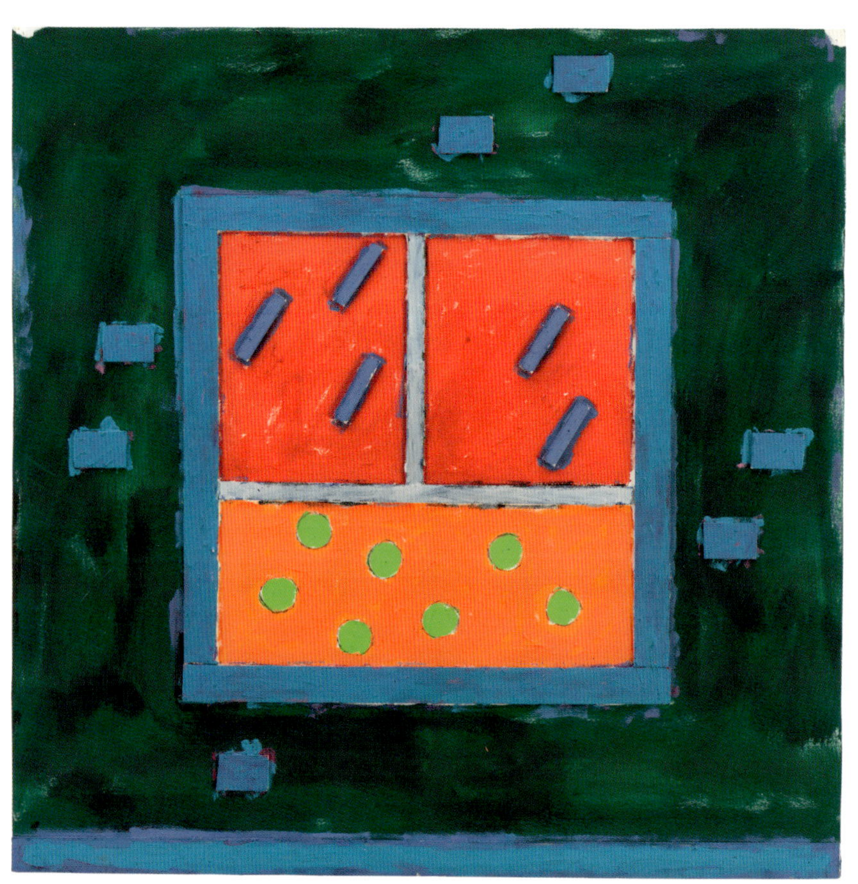

Untitled (Study for *Night Moods*), 1983

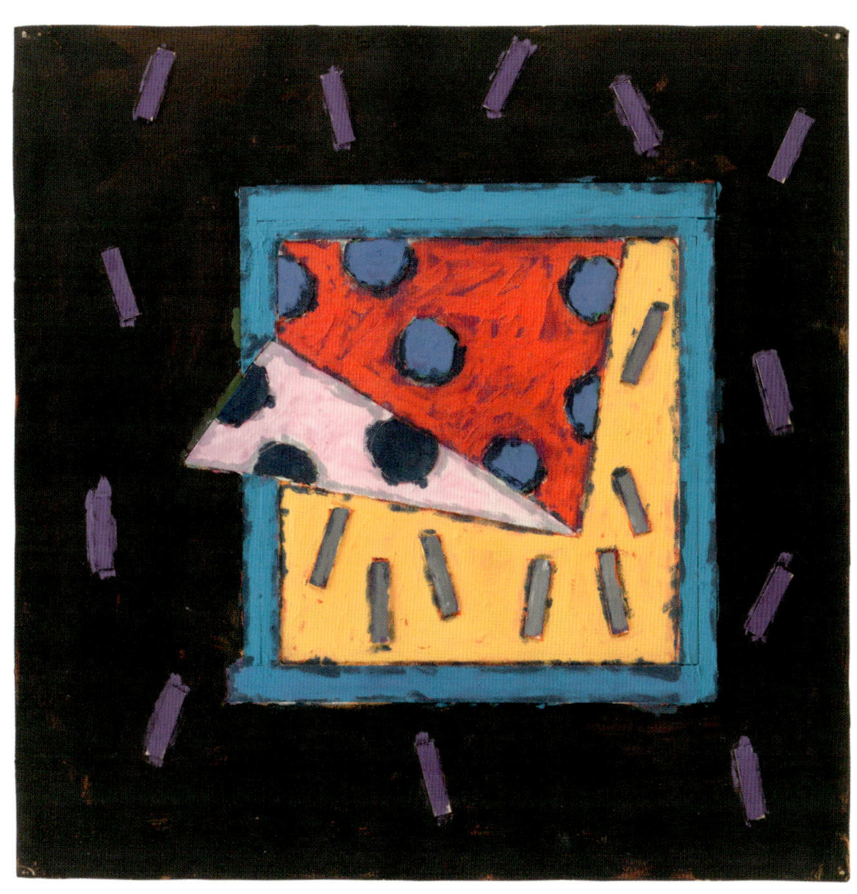

Untitled (Study for *Night Moods*), 1983

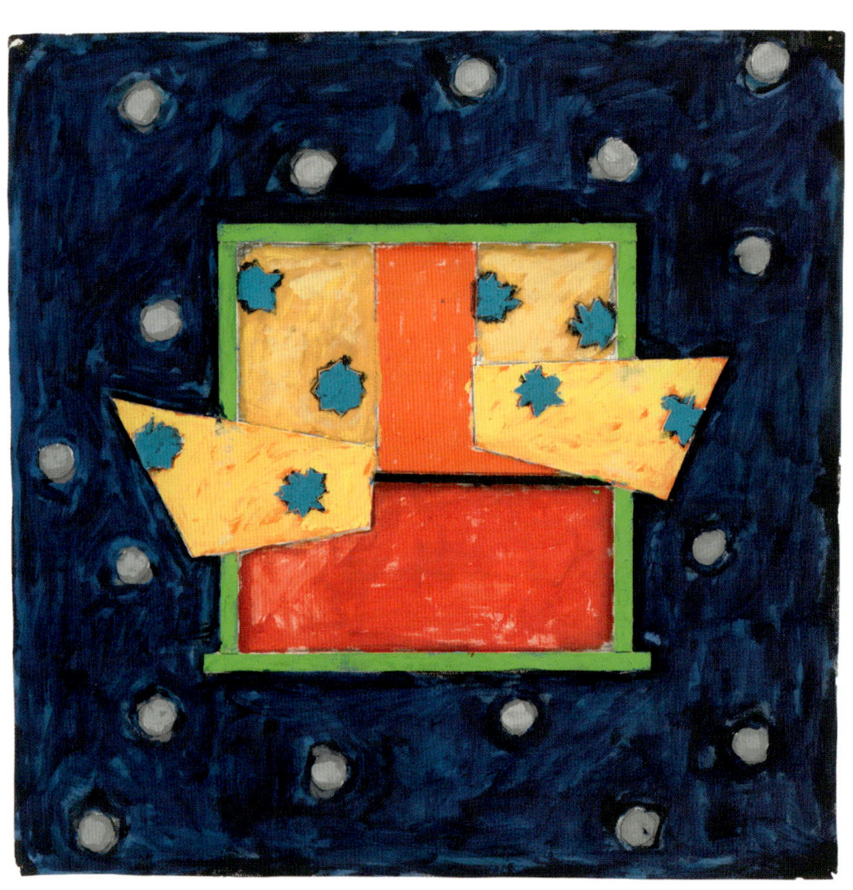

Untitled (Study for *Night Moods*), 1983

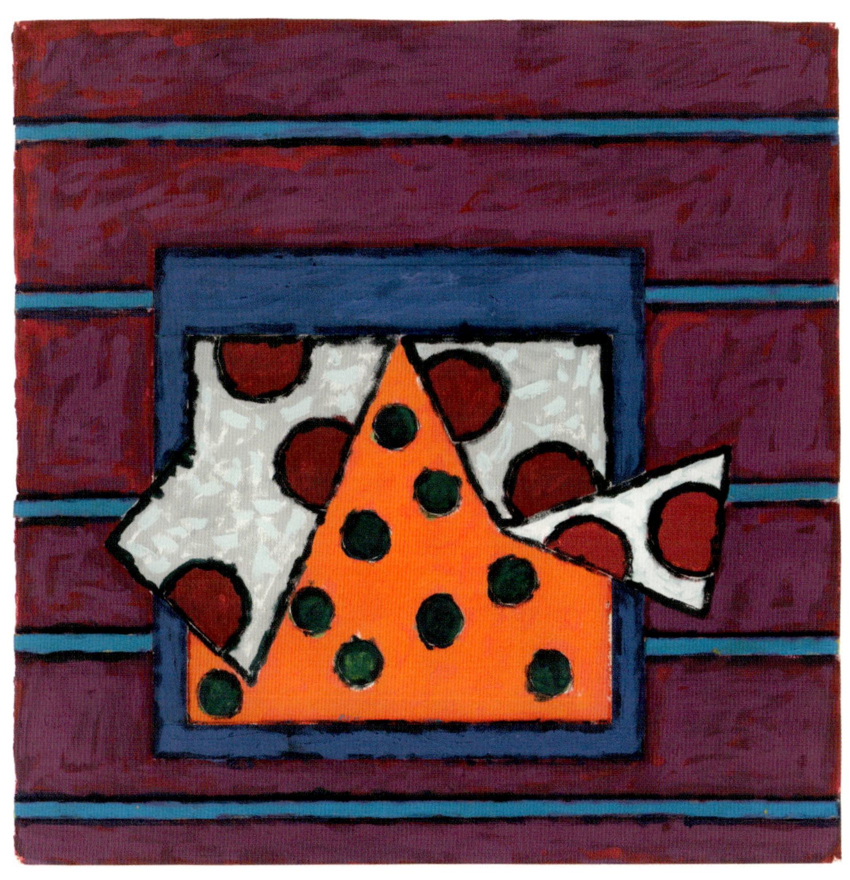

Untitled (Study for *Night Moods*), 1983

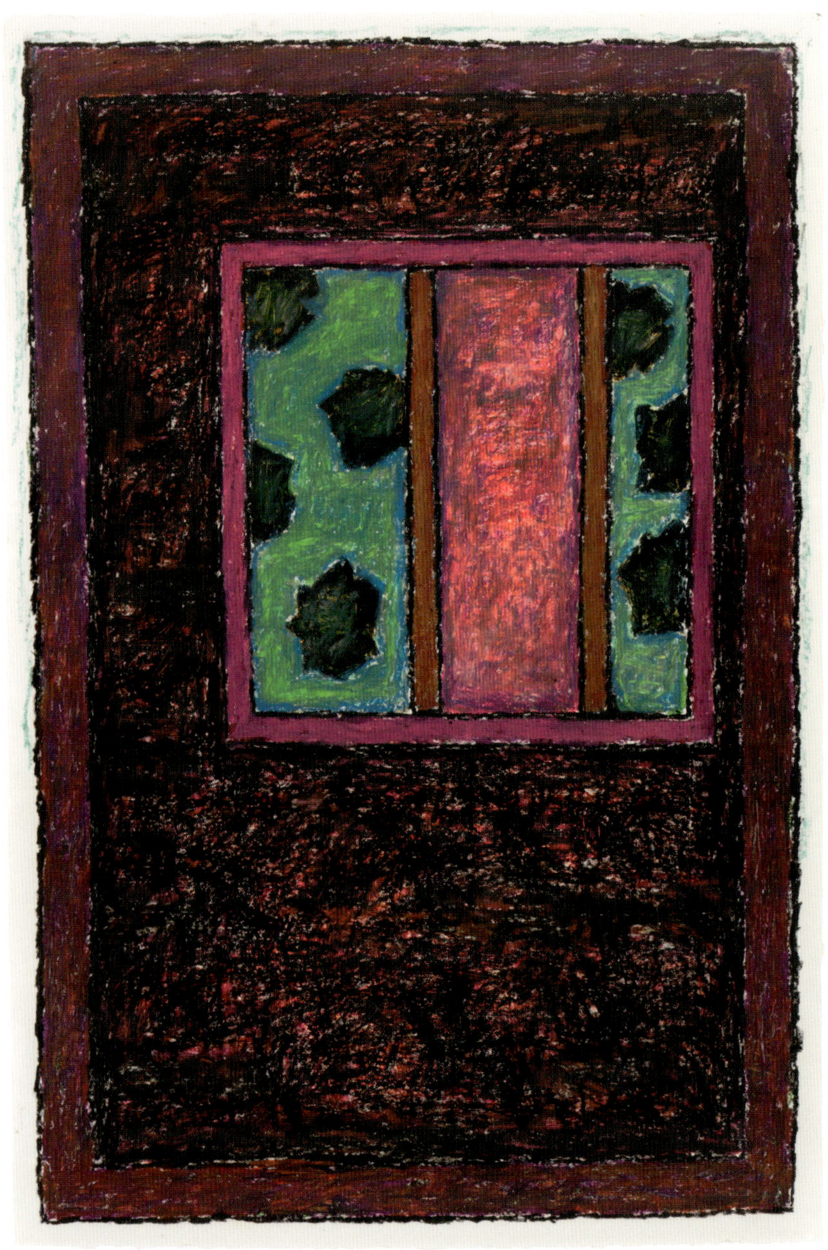

Untitled, 1984

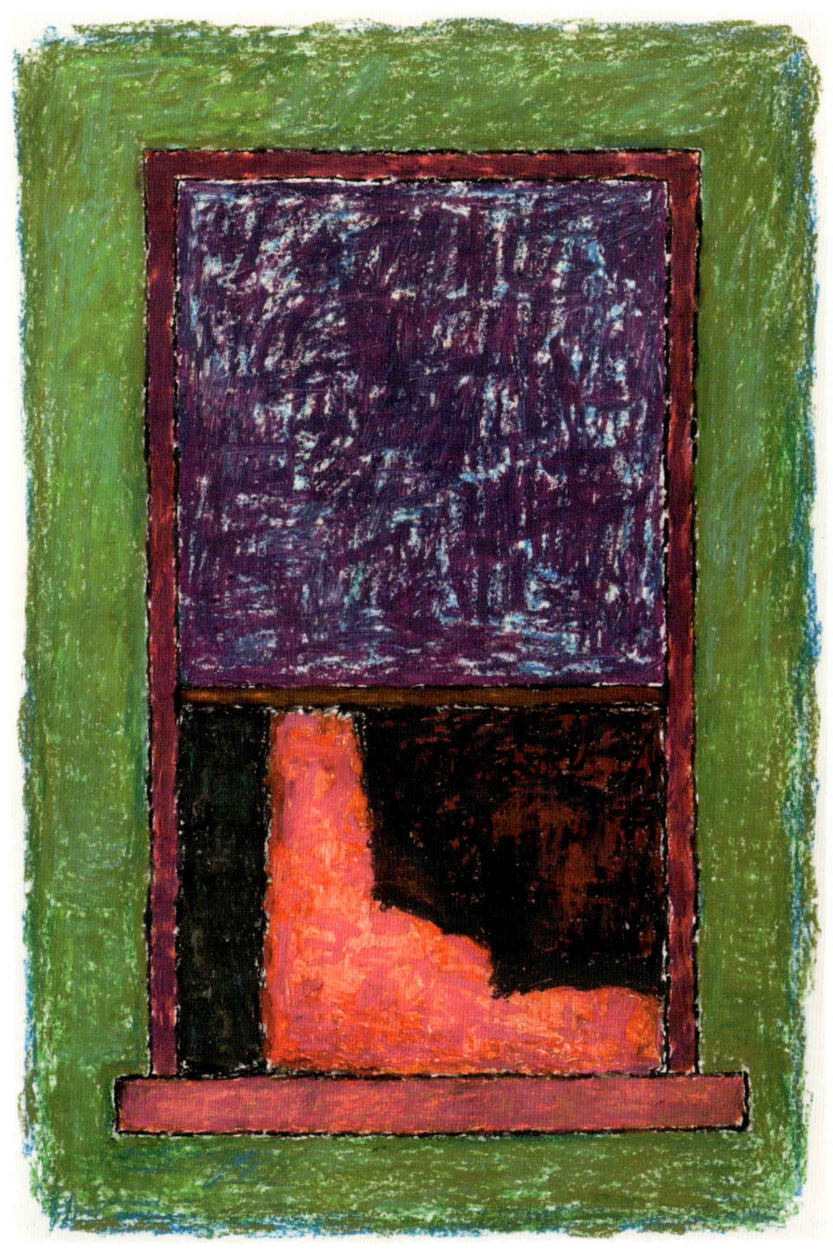

Untitled, 1984

SHAPE
EQUALS
CONTENT

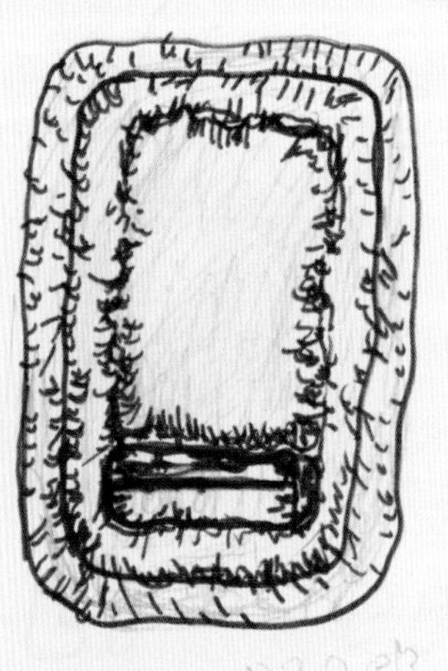

IT IS,
AND SHOULD
CREATE
REAL
SPACE

BLACK

D
PENCIL
AND
PEN

BOUNDARIES
FINDING THE LIMITS
OF MY WORLD = KNOWING
MY WORLD

TO
PURE ABSTACTION

Ralph Humphrey: Framed, Framing

Klaus Kertess

In 1963, as my first year in graduate school at Yale was drawing to a close, Egbert Haverkamp-Begemann, the head of the art history department, invited me into his office to discuss my future plans. I had, in one year, been a teacher's assistant, written a master's thesis, and taken a full course load. I had arrived in graduate school torn between fifteenth-century Florence and twentieth-century modernism. The latter had won, and I had decided that the most exciting pursuit for me would be to open a gallery representing contemporary artists who would put me in visceral contact with the process of creating. Haverkamp-Begemann was stunned when I told him this. In his eyes, I would be nothing without a doctorate. But I wasn't budging. He kept telling me I was wasting a major opportunity to further my career. When I could no longer take the growing volume of his harangue, I got up and excused myself.

I moved to New York and went to work for Interpublic, at that time the world's largest and most successful advertising agency. Marion Harper was the reigning genius of this vast organization, and he had early in my life told me he wanted me to work for him. My father was Marion's "intellectual friend," and I became his surrogate son. At Interpublic, I was paid well but had no tasks to perform. Almost daily, I arrived with an attaché case containing that day's *New York Times* and a bathing suit. I read the paper, then walked to a nearby hotel that had a large swimming pool I could pay to swim in. Buster Crabbe, an All-American swimmer and star of the film *Tarzan the Fearless* (1933), joined me almost every day. I never actually saw him swim. He was usually sweating away in the steam room and seldom spoke other than to tell me over and over again how lucky I was to be young enough to make the mistakes necessary to start my life. He was thirty years older than me but seemed to have no occupation other than his daily steam. After my swim, I would either walk the length of 57th Street and back or walk up Madison Avenue as far as art galleries were still located. The art world was then comprised of 57th Street and Madison Avenue. At that time, one could see almost every exhibition in New York over the course of one week's lunch breaks. At Yale, I had been introduced to Willem de Kooning's work and found it too slovenly, not having a clue how much time and enthusiasm I would later devote to his work. However, Jackson Pollock, whose paintings were far more difficult to absorb than de Kooning's, had already claimed territory in my memory's front yard. I had never seen anything as empty as Robert Ryman's all-white paintings with their strict white surfaces and occasional metal mounts for attaching the painting to the wall. Robert Mangold, Richard Serra, Agnes Martin, John Chamberlain, and others also practiced their subversive seduction on me.

Among the most perplexing of the galleries I visited was the Green Gallery, run by the legendary Dick Bellamy. There, I saw Dan Flavin's early light pieces, multipart paintings by James Rosenquist, and Lucas Samaras padding about in his underwear in the vicinity of the cubicle he had built for himself to inhabit for the duration of his exhibition. However, the most confounding exhibition I saw at the Green Gallery was Ralph Humphrey's.

Some six or seven paintings, each about four feet high and six feet wide, filled the gallery space with mournful wails. Each painting had a restrained interior frame, around five or six inches wide, enclosing a monochrome gray interior. The color of the frame varied from painting to painting—a subdued pale blue, a dirty yellow, an almost salmon red. I stood consternated waiting for one or another of the paintings to reveal itself to me; but each remained ungiving. Why, I wondered, would anyone make a muted gray emptiness the central event of his painting? I left exasperated. Humphrey's exhibition, I knew, would be the last before the Green Gallery closed. Torn between dismay and aroused curiosity, I returned to the gallery every lunchtime for a week, only to feel more and more antagonized by the artist's strange undertaking. The last time I went, I tried to glue myself to the floor as I confronted the gray. I stood trying to stare it down for quite some time. Suddenly, I realized I was being framed. I had been vaporized and ushered into grayness to examine myself in the context of that grayness. I needed to learn to create a frame for myself.

It was at this time that I decided to open my own gallery. Jeff Byers, a good friend from my undergraduate years at Yale, had decided to fund it, and I would now need to find six or seven artists to represent. I asked the few people I knew in the art world if they knew how to contact Ralph Humphrey, but got nowhere. I knew Henry Geldzahler, the Metropolitan Museum's curator of contemporary art and one of the high priests of the contemporary scene. I spent an hour with him in his office discussing my ideas for the gallery. He encouraged me and offered to help in any way he could.

On a whim several days later, I picked up the New York City phone book and looked up "Humphrey, Ralph," and there it was. My right hand shook so much that I could barely dial the number. A slightly high-pitched, intense voice answered. It was Ralph Humphrey. I told him his show at Green had amazed me, made me see in a new way. I wanted to visit him in his studio but he said we should meet somewhere else first. I do not remember where we met the next day; I only remember that Ralph was agitated and a bit stunned when I told him I was starting a gallery and could think of no better artist to head up our then non-existent roster than him. He blustered some but calmed down when I asked him to describe his process of making a painting. At the end of our meeting, Ralph said he would need to think about my proposal and asked if we could meet again in a month. He thanked me and left. I would agonize for the next month, wondering what his decision would be.

Several weeks later, on April 27, 1966, I attended the opening of the *Primary Structures* show at the Jewish Museum, then presenting some of the most important contemporary art exhibitions. I had gotten to know a few artists, and one of them, Carlos Villa, a gregarious painter of Filipino origins, had perhaps the thickest address book of the art world. Carlos asked me whom I would really like in the gallery, and without hesitation I responded "Ralph Humphrey." "If you like Humphrey, you'll really like Brice Marden," he said, and then led me up to the second floor where Marden was leaning against a vitrine of rare Judaica. He was a bit drunk but we managed to make an appointment for the next day. When he opened the door to his studio, my eyes initially swept by him and focused instead on an ambiguous beacon of gray that radiated on the wall. Approximately five months later, on September 20, 1966, the Bykert Gallery would open on 57th Street, in the space previously occupied by the Green Gallery. The gallery name was an awkward amalgam of Jeff's and my names but would slowly accumulate meaning over the next nine years, much of it emanating from Ralph Humphrey's and Brice Marden's paintings.

My relationship with Ralph was sporadic but intense. Typically, I would see his new paintings just a few days before the movers would pick them up and bring them to the gallery to be hung for his exhibitions. His studio was across the hall from the apartment he shared with his wife Karen and daughter Beth, on Manhattan's Upper West Side. Occasionally, Ralph would have me over to dinner. Tension reigned during those meals. Afterward, however, Ralph and I would adjourn to his studio and, once more, his painting would overwhelm me.

Ralph also had an intense relationship with his colors. He inhabited them. He could hold forth on green, at length, even though he seldom employed it in his work. And he was quite smitten with the directors of French New Wave cinema. He particularly admired Claude Chabrol and the erotic suspense that pervaded his best films. And like so many others, including myself, Ralph was deeply taken with Michelangelo Antonioni's

Blow Up (1966). The layered ambiguities and tensions so prominent in the work of these directors paralleled the shifting space and configuration that so frequently enlivens Ralph's paintings. Antonioni, in particular, had a painterly bent that went as far as having the grass in *Blow Up* tinted a green to his camera lens' liking.

Ralph's first exhibition at the Bykert Gallery took place early in 1967 and comprised a number of paintings, each with three thin parallel bands traversing the width of the painting. The bands had been painted with a mixture of Day-Glo and acrylic paints and gave off a kind of gaseous visual buzz that activated the neutral gray ground. They were imbued with magical mystery. To my happy amazement, the exhibition sold out very quickly. Two days after the last painting was spoken for, Ralph burst into the gallery exclaiming, "What's wrong with my paintings?" I had expected thanks, not an interrogation. After a few more outbursts, I realized Ralph's defense system was based on his conviction that his paintings were too good for the ordinary collector to understand or covet, so that a sold out exhibition could only mean his work had actually taken a turn for the worse. I proposed this to him, and he begrudgingly accepted it. Ralph was fragile, often defensive about his impoverished background. His father was a coal miner and his mother abusive. Somehow his parents had filled him with enough shame so that success did not seem to be an option for him.

In more settled moments, Ralph might speak at length about Matisse's cutouts or Morandi. Rothko would also be brought up. Rothko had been a major influence on Ralph, and they were friends. However, Ralph seems to have inherited some Abstract Expressionist paranoia from Rothko. When Rothko did not appear at one of Ralph's openings, he was distraught and wondered what he had done to annoy his friend. When Rothko appeared in the gallery a week later, he pointedly let me know that he had not received an announcement, and I could not convince him to save his ire for the United States Postal Service.

After Ralph's death, quite a few notebooks were found in his studio, more often than not filled with lists and drawings for his paintings. Seldom is a complete sentence to be found, and there are many misspellings. Often he created his lists with exaggerated bubble script that leavened his usual seriousness with the comic. A broken phrase from a Janis Joplin song, "Freedom . . . nothing left to loose," might succeed "Work will fluctuate in its forward space." A few pages on, in large bubble letters, "Power, force, immediacy, completeness, unity, realized" consume a whole page. Elsewhere, "Shape equals content." A little further on, "Art is the life, the life is art." And so it was for Ralph.

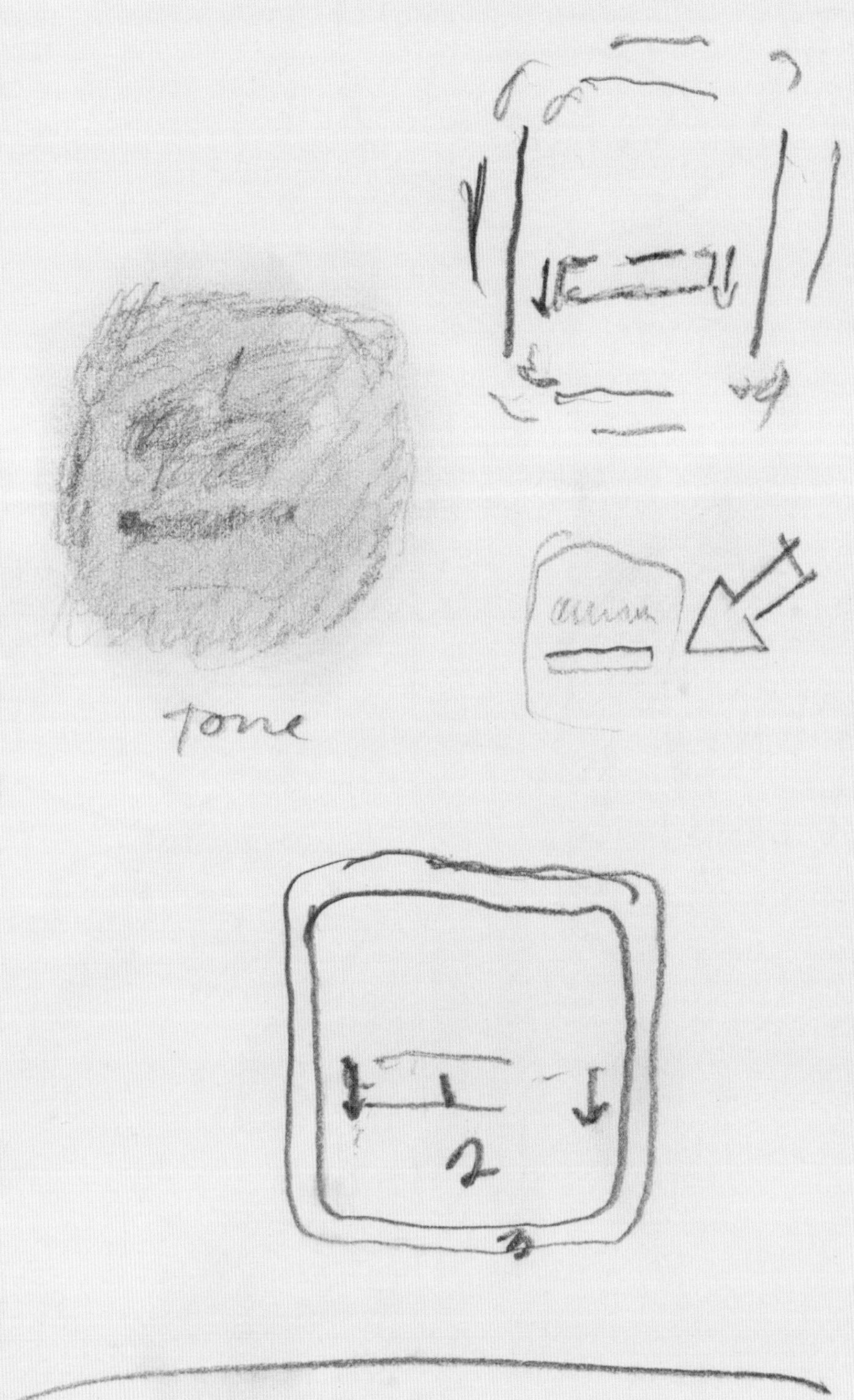
tone
2

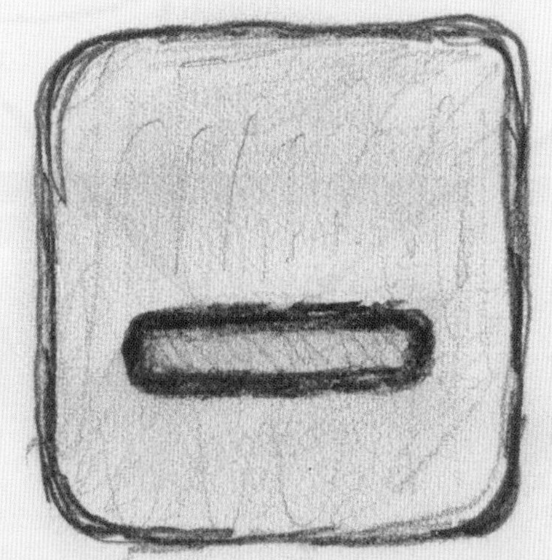

SINCLAIR

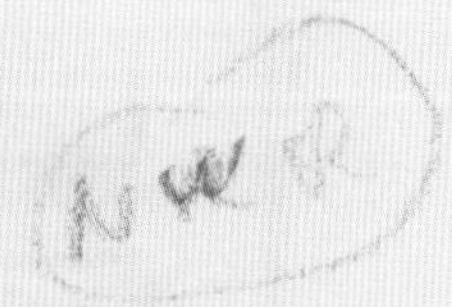

SINCLAIR

Catalogue

PAINTINGS

page 2: *Shuttle*, 1981
Casein and modeling paste on wood
24 x 24 3/4 x 6 inches

page 4: *Untitled*, 1975–1976
Casein and modeling paste on canvas
36 x 48 x 8 inches

page 7: *Untitled*, 1985–1987
Casein and modeling paste on wood
60 x 54 x 2 3/4 inches

page 9: *Untitled*, 1973
Casein and modeling paste on canvas
96 x 50 x 6 inches

page 11: *Untitled*, 1975
Casein and modeling paste on canvas
60 x 72 x 5 1/2 inches

page 13: *Conveyance #4*, 1976–1977
Casein and modeling paste on wood
60 x 36 x 10 inches

page 15: *For Norman*, 1977
Casein and modeling paste on canvas
48 x 48 x 6 inches

page 17: *Untitled*, 1977
Casein and modeling paste on wood
48 x 48 x 6 inches

page 19: *Flamingo*, 1979
Casein and modeling paste on wood
48 x 48 x 4 inches

page 21: *Guided Tour*, 1979
Casein and modeling paste on wood
70 x 36 x 8 inches

page 23: *Christmas Story*, 1979–1980
Casein and modeling paste on wood
42 x 84 x 7 inches

page 25: *Thin Edge*, 1981
Casein and modeling paste on canvas and wood
60 x 36 x 4 inches

page 27: *Heat*, 1983–1984
Casein and modeling paste on canvas and wood
60 x 36 x 6 1/2 inches

page 29: *Untitled*, 1983–1984
Casein and modeling paste on wood
48 x 54 x 2 1/4 inches

page 31: *Screens*, 1983–1984
Casein and modeling paste on wood
48 x 48 x 2 1/4 inches

page 33: *Mountain*, 1983–1984
Casein and modeling paste on wood
60 x 36 x 4 inches

page 35: *Forest*, 1984
Casein and modeling paste on wood
60 x 90 x 3 inches

page 37: *Desert*, 1984
Casein and modeling paste on wood
48 x 48 x 2 1/4 inches

page 39: *Border*, 1984
Casein and modeling paste on wood
60 x 84 x 3 inches

DRAWINGS

page 44: *Untitled*, 1973
Casein and watercolor on paper
7 1/8 x 10 1/4 inches

page 45: *Untitled*, 1976
Casein on paper collage
12 x 16 inches

page 46: *Untitled*, 1980
Ink, graphite, and chalk on velvet
20 x 26 inches

page 47: *Untitled*, c. 1979–1980
Casein, velvet, and paper collage on velvet
20 x 22 inches

page 48: *Untitled* (Study for *Night Moods*), 1983
Casein, graphite, wood, and paper collage on paper
23 3/4 x 24 inches

page 49: *Untitled* (Study for *Night Moods*), 1983
Casein, graphite, wood, and paper collage on paper
23 3/4 x 24 inches

page 50: *Untitled* (Study for *Night Moods*), 1983
Casein, graphite, wood, and paper collage on paper
23 3/4 x 24 inches

page 51: *Untitled* (Study for *Night Moods*), 1983
Casein, graphite, wood, and paper collage on paper
23 3/4 x 24 inches

page 52: *Untitled*, 1984
Pastel on paper
44 x 30 inches

page 53: *Untitled*, 1984
Pastel on paper
44 x 30 inches

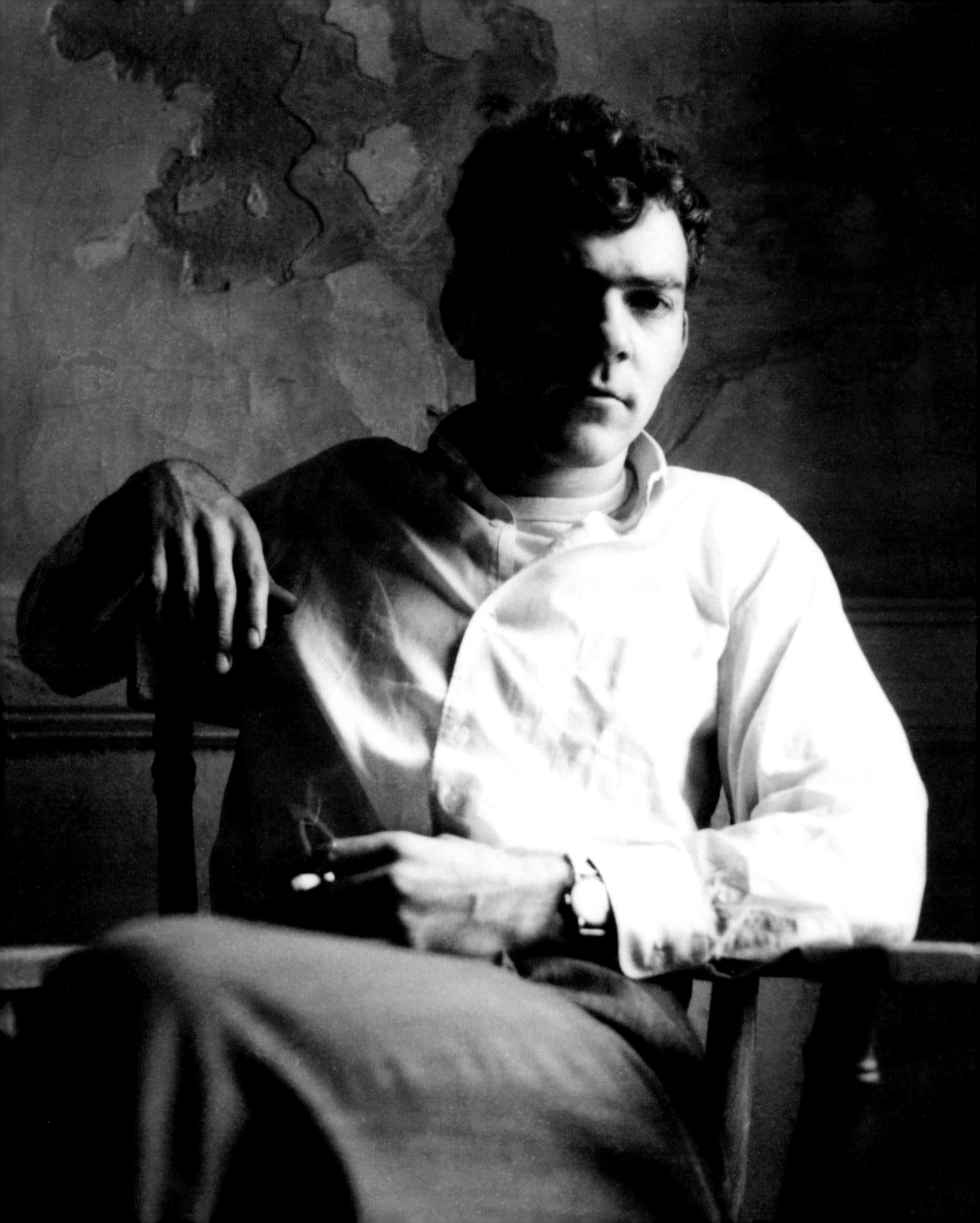

Biography

1932
Born: Youngstown, Ohio

1990
Died: New York, New York

EDUCATION

1951–1952, 1954–1956
Youngstown University, Ohio

TEACHING

1966–1990
Professor, Hunter College, City University of New York

SELECTED SOLO EXHIBITIONS

1959
Ralph Humphrey, Tibor de Nagy Gallery, New York, February 3–21

1960
Ralph Humphrey, Tibor de Nagy Gallery, New York, February 2–21

1961
Ralph Humphrey: Recent Paintings, Mayer Gallery, New York, March 14–April 1

1965
Ralph Humphrey, Green Gallery, New York, May 5–29

1967
Ralph Humphrey, Bykert Gallery, New York, January 10–February 24

1968
Ralph Humphrey, Bykert Gallery, New York, February 3–29

1969
Ralph Humphrey, Bykert Gallery, New York, February 1–27
Galerie Alfred Schmela, Düsseldorf

1970
Ralph Humphrey, Bykert Gallery, New York, April 4–25

1971
Ralph Humphrey, André Emmerich Gallery, New York, March 20–April 8

1972
Ralph Humphrey, Bykert Gallery, New York, May 2–23

1973
Ralph Humphrey, Bykert Gallery, New York, May 12–June 2
Ralph Humphrey: Survey of Paintings, Texas Gallery, Houston, May 15–June 9

1974
Ralph Humphrey, Bykert Gallery, New York, April 20–May 15
Ralph Humphrey: Paintings, Daniel Weinberg Gallery, San Francisco, November–December

1975

Ralph Humphrey: Paintings, 1974, Bykert Gallery, New York, February 4–26

Ralph Humphrey: Paintings, 1958–1966, Bykert/Downtown, New York, February 4–26

1976

Ralph Humphrey, John Weber Gallery, New York, January 31–February 25

1976–1977

Ralph Humphrey: Recent Paintings, Daniel Weinberg Gallery, San Francisco, December 16, 1976–January 22, 1977

1977

Ralph Humphrey, John Weber Gallery, New York, February 9–26

1980

Ralph Humphrey, Willard Gallery, New York, April 5–May 7

1982

Ralph Humphrey, Willard Gallery, New York, April 3–May 8

Ralph Humphrey: Paintings, 1975–1982, Daniel Weinberg Gallery, Los Angeles, October 6–30

1983

Ralph Humphrey: Selected Paintings, Daniel Weinberg Gallery, Los Angeles, May 14–June 11

1984

Delahunty Gallery, Dallas

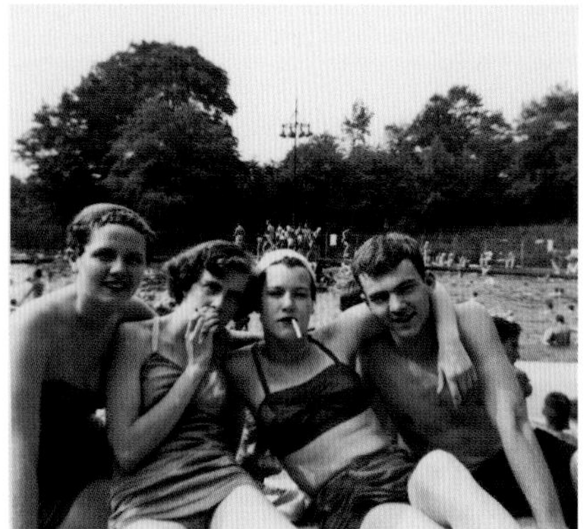

Ralph Humphrey, Willard Gallery, New York, April 7–May 12

1985

Ralph Humphrey: Recent Paintings, Daniel Weinberg Gallery, Los Angeles, October 16–November 2

1987

Ralph Humphrey, Jay Gorney Modern Art, New York, January–February

1990

Ralph Humphrey: 1990, Mary Boone Gallery, New York, March 3–31

Ralph Humphrey: Frame Paintings, 1964 to 1965, Mary Boone Gallery, New York, September 8–October 6

Ralph Humphrey: A Retrospective View, 1954–1990, Daniel Weinberg Gallery, Los Angeles, November 8–December 5

1991

Ralph Humphrey: The Late Paintings on Paper, Bertha and Karl Leubsdorf Art Gallery, Hunter College, City University of New York, September 19–October 26

Ralph Humphrey: Paintings, 1975–1985, John Berggruen Gallery, San Francisco, October–November

1996

Ralph Humphrey: Selected Paintings, Daniel Weinberg Gallery, San Francisco, August 17–October 17

1998

Ralph Humphrey, Danese Gallery, New York, January 16–February 14

2000

Ralph Humphrey: Early Paintings, 1957–1967, Daniel Weinberg Gallery, Los Angeles, November 1–December 9

2001

Ralph Humphrey: Later Paintings, 1975–1982, Daniel Weinberg Gallery, Los Angeles, April 5–May 26

2008

Ralph Humphrey: Selected Works from the Estate, Nielsen Gallery, Boston, May 17–June 14

Ralph Humphrey: Selected Paintings, 1957–1980, Daniel Weinberg Gallery, Los Angeles, May 31–June 28

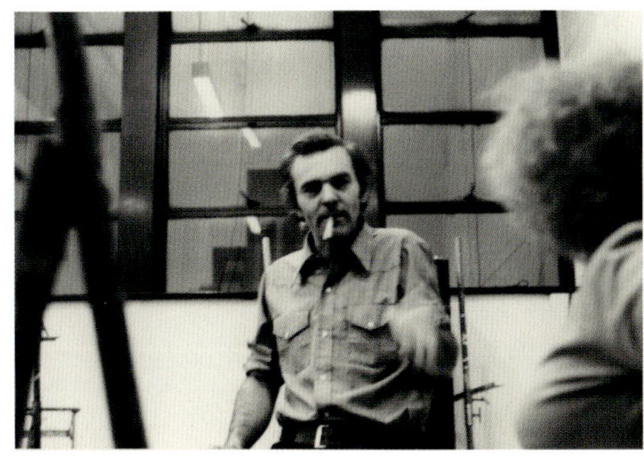

SELECTED GROUP EXHIBITIONS

1961

American Abstract Expressionists and Imagists, Solomon R. Guggenheim Museum, New York, October–December

1966

Systemic Painting, Solomon R. Guggenheim Museum, New York, September–November

1967

Selected N.Y.C. Artists 1967, Ithaca College Museum of Art, Ithaca, New York, April 4–May 27

Focus on Light, New Jersey State Museum, Trenton, May 20–September 10

Highlights of the 1966–1967 Art Season, Aldrich Museum of Contemporary Art, Ridgefield, Connecticut, June 18–September 4

A Romantic Minimalism, Institute of Contemporary Art, University of Pennsylvania, Philadelphia, September 13–October 11

1968

Bykert Gallery, New York

The Art of the Real: USA, 1948–1968, Museum of Modern Art, New York, July 3–September 8

1968–1969

The Pure and Clear: American Innovations, Philadelphia Museum of Art, November 13, 1968–January 21, 1969

1969

American Painting: The 1960s, Georgia Museum of Art, University of Georgia, Athens, September 22–November 8

Current Minimal Painting, Vassar College Art Gallery, Poughkeepsie, New York

1969–1970

1969 Annual Exhibition: Contemporary American Painting, Whitney Museum of American Art, New York, December 16, 1969–February 1, 1970

1970–1971

Color and Field, 1890–1970, Albright-Knox Art Gallery, Buffalo, September 15–November 1, 1970; Dayton Art Institute, Ohio, November 20, 1970–January 10, 1971; Cleveland Museum of Art, February 4–March 28, 1971

1971

The Structure of Color, Whitney Museum of American Art, New York, February 25–April 18

Spray, Santa Barbara Museum of Art, California, April 24–May 30

Bykert Gallery, New York

Art of the Decade, 1960–1970: Paintings from the Collections of Greater Detroit, University Art Gallery, Oakland University, Rochester, Michigan, November 14–December 17

1972

Painting and Sculpture Today, Indianapolis Museum of Art, April 26–June 4

Current American Abstract Painting, Vassar College Art Gallery, Poughkeepsie, New York

Dealers' Choice, La Jolla Museum of Contemporary Art, California, July 15–September 27

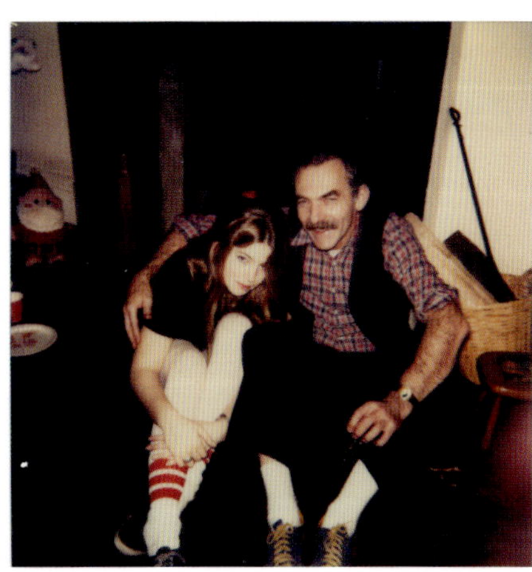

1973

Drawings, Bykert Gallery, New York, January 6–24

Gallery Toselli, Milan

1974

New Painting: Stressing Surface, Katonah Gallery, Katonah, New York, May 4–June 23

Painting and Sculpture Today, Indianapolis Museum of Art, May 22–July 14; Taft Museum of Art, Cincinnati, September 12–October 24

Ten Painters in New York, Michael Walls Gallery, New York, June 15–July 6

Seventy-First American Exhibition, Art Institute of Chicago, June 15–August 11

1975

22 Artists, Susan Caldwell Gallery, New York, January 4–25

Fourteen Abstract Painters, Frederick S. Wight Art Gallery, University of California, Los Angeles, March 25–May 25

Fourteen Artists, Baltimore Museum of Art, April 15–June 1

A Group Show Selected by Klaus Kertess, Texas Gallery, Houston, September 15–October 11

Douglas Drake Gallery, Kansas City, Missouri

1975–1976

Painting, Drawing, and Sculpture of the '60s and '70s from the Dorothy and Herbert Vogel Collection, Institute of Contemporary Art, University of Pennsylvania, Philadelphia, October 7–November 18, 1975; Contemporary Arts Center, Cincinnati, December 17, 1975–February 15, 1976

1976

Ideas on Paper: 1970–1976, Renaissance Society at the University of Chicago, May 2–June 6

Daniel Weinberg Gallery, San Francisco

1977

Paintings on Paper, Drawing Center, New York, January 15–26

Galerie Jean-Paul Najar, Paris

'75, '76, '77: Painting, Part I, Sarah Lawrence College Art Gallery, Bronxville, New York, February 19–March 10; American Foundation for the Arts, Miami, April–May; Contemporary Arts Center, Cincinnati, June–July

A View of a Decade, Museum of Contemporary Art, Chicago, September 10–November 10

John Weber Gallery, New York

1977–1978

Works from the Collection of Dorothy and Herbert Vogel, University of Michigan Museum of Art, Ann Arbor, November 11, 1977–January 1, 1978

1978–1979

Late Twentieth Century Art from the Sydney and Frances Lewis Foundation, Anderson Gallery, Virginia Commonwealth University, Richmond, December 5, 1978–January 9, 1979; Institute of Contemporary Art, University of Pennsylvania, Philadelphia, March 22–May 2, 1979

1979

1979 Biennial Exhibition, Whitney Museum of American Art, New York, February 6–April 1

Generation, Susan Caldwell Gallery, New York

The Reductive Object: A Survey of the Minimalist Aesthetic in the 1960s, Institute of Contemporary Art, Boston, March 7–April 29

The Implicit Image: Abstract Painting in the '70s, Nielsen Gallery, Boston, April 29–June 1

Color and Structure, Hamilton Gallery, New York, May 5–June 2

Texas Gallery, Houston

1980

Black, White, Other, R.H. Oosterom Gallery, New York, January 17–February 17

Current/New York: Recent Works in Relief, Joe and Emily Lowe Art Gallery, Syracuse University, Syracuse, New York, January 27–February 24

Painting in Relief, Whitney Museum of American Art, Downtown Branch, New York, January 30–March 5

Painting and Sculpture Today, Indianapolis Museum of Art, June 24–August 17

3 Dimensional Painting, Museum of Contemporary Art, Chicago, August 2–November 9

Planar Painting: Constructs, 1975–1980, Alternative Museum, New York, October 18–November 15, 1980

The Image Transformed, Art Latitude Gallery, New York, November 4–29

1981

A Seventies Selection: An Exhibition of Works from the Collection of the Whitney Museum of American Art, Miami University Art Museum, Oxford, Ohio, February 14–June 14

Abstract Mythologies, Nielsen Gallery, Boston, March 1–31
Between Painting and Sculpture, Pam Adler Gallery, New York, March 31–April 25

1981–1982
Drawing Invitational 1981, Harm Bouckaert Gallery, New York, December 2, 1981–January 2, 1982

1982
The Erotic Impulse, Roger Litz Gallery, New York
Postminimalism, Aldrich Museum of Contemporary Art, Ridgefield, Connecticut, September 19–December 19

1983
Abstract Painting: 1960–1969, P.S. 1 Contemporary Art Center, Queens, January 16–March 13
New Work, New York: Newcastle Salutes New York, Newcastle Polytechnic Gallery, Newcastle-upon-Tyne, United Kingdom, October 8–November 4

1984
Parasol and Simca: Two Presses/Two Processes, Center Gallery, Bucknell University, Lewisburg, Pennsylvania, February 3–April 4, 1984; Sordoni Art Gallery, Wilkes College, Wilkes-Barre, Pennsylvania, April 15–May 13
The Meditative Surface, Renaissance Society at the University of Chicago, April 1–May 16

1985
Abstract Painting Redefined, Louis K. Meisel Gallery, New York, February 16–March 30
Now and Then: A Selection of Recent and Earlier Paintings, Daniel Weinberg Gallery, Los Angeles, June 1–August 31
American Abstract Painting: 1960–1980, Margo Leavin Gallery, Los Angeles, June 19–August 24

1986
The Purist Image, Marian Locks Gallery, Philadelphia, November

1986–1987
The Window in Twentieth-Century Art, Neuberger Museum of Art, Purchase College, State University of New York, September 21, 1986–January 18, 1987; Contemporary Arts Museum, Houston, April 24–June 29, 1987

1997
A Lasting Legacy: Selections from the Lannan Foundation Gift, Museum of Contemporary Art, Los Angeles, September 9–December 14

2004
A Minimal Future?: Art as Object, 1958–1968, Museum of Contemporary Art, Los Angeles, March 28–July 26

2006–2007
High Times, Hard Times: New York Painting, 1967–1975, Weatherspoon Art Museum, University of North Carolina, Greensboro, August 6–October 15, 2006; American University Museum at the Katzen Arts Center, American University, Washington, D.C., November 21, 2006–January 21, 2007; National Academy Museum, New York, February 13–April 27, 2007

2008
The Idea of Nature, 33 Bond Gallery, New York, June 12–July 31
Into the Void: Abstract Art, 1948–2008, Tucson Museum of Art, July 17–September 26

2008–2009
Steve DiBenedetto, Ralph Humphrey, Chris Martin, and Andrew Masullo/Paintings, Daniel Weinberg Gallery, Los Angeles, December 6, 2008–January 31, 2009

2009
Image Matter, Mary Boone Gallery, New York, February 21–March 28
Not New: Vincent Fecteau Selects from the Collection, San Francisco Museum of Modern Art, July 25–November 8

2010
Wall-to-Wall, Daniel Weinberg Gallery, Los Angeles, June 5–August 14

2011
Surface Truths: Abstract Painting in the Sixties, Norton Simon Museum, Pasadena, California, March 25–August 15

2011–2012
The Language of Less: Then and Now, Museum of Contemporary Art, Chicago, October 8, 2011–April 8, 2012

2012

Susan Hartnett, Ralph Humphrey, Marilyn Lerner, and Dona Nelson, Mary Boone Gallery, New York, March 22–April 28

SELECTED MUSEUM COLLECTIONS

Addison Gallery of American Art, Phillips Academy, Andover, Massachusetts
Allen Memorial Art Museum, Oberlin College, Ohio
Butler Institute of American Art, Youngstown, Ohio
Carnegie Museum of Art, Pittsburgh
Dayton Art Institute, Ohio
Miami Art Museum
Museum of Contemporary Art, Chicago
Museum of Contemporary Art, Los Angeles
Museum of Contemporary Art, San Diego
Museum of Fine Arts, Boston
Museum of Fine Arts, Houston
Museum of Modern Art, New York
National Gallery of Australia, Canberra
Norton Simon Museum, Pasadena, California
Oklahoma City Museum of Art
Palm Springs Art Museum
Parrish Art Museum, Southampton, New York
Philadelphia Museum of Art
Rose Art Museum, Brandeis University, Waltham, Massachusetts
San Francisco Museum of Modern Art
Smithsonian American Art Museum, Washington, D.C.
Tucson Museum of Art
Virginia Museum of Fine Arts, Richmond
Walker Art Center, Minneapolis
Weatherspoon Art Museum, University of North Carolina, Greensboro
Whitney Museum of American Art, New York

Selected Bibliography

BOOKS AND CATALOGUES

Aldrich Museum of Contemporary Art. *Highlights of the 1966–67 Art Season*. Ridgefield, CT: Aldrich Museum of Contemporary Art, 1967.

Alloway, Lawrence. *Systemic Painting*. New York: Solomon R. Guggenheim Museum, 1966.

Art Gallery, Oakland University. *Art of the Decade: 1960–1970*. Rochester, MI: Art Gallery, Oakland University, 1971.

Art Institute of Chicago. *Seventy-First American Exhibition*. Chicago: Art Institute of Chicago, 1974.

Baltimore Museum of Art. *Fourteen Artists*. Baltimore: Baltimore Museum of Art, 1975.

Bellamy, Richard. *Focus on Light*. Trenton: New Jersey State Museum, 1967.

Bertha and Karl Leubsdorf Art Gallery, Hunter College, City University of New York. *Ralph Humphrey: The Late Paintings on Paper*. New York: Bertha and Karl Leubsdorf Art Gallery, Hunter College, City University of New York, 1991.

Colt, Priscilla. *Color and Field: 1890–1970*. Buffalo: Albright-Knox Art Gallery, 1970.

Contemporary Art Society. *Painting and Sculpture Today*. Indianapolis: Indianapolis Museum of Art, 1972.

Contemporary Art Society. *Painting and Sculpture Today*. Indianapolis: Indianapolis Museum of Art, 1974.

Contemporary Art Society. *Painting and Sculpture Today*. Indianapolis: Indianapolis Museum of Art, 1980.

Danese Gallery. *Ralph Humphrey*. New York: Danese Gallery, 1998.

Darling, Michael. *The Language of Less: Then and Now*. Chicago: Museum of Contemporary Art, 2011.

Delehanty, Suzanne. *The Window in Twentieth-Century Art*. Purchase, NY: Neuberger Museum of Art, Purchase College, State University of New York, 1986.

Friedman, Martin L. *A View of a Decade*. Chicago: Museum of Contemporary Art, 1977.

Goldstein, Ann. *A Lasting Legacy: Selections from the Lannan Foundation Gift*. Los Angeles: Museum of Contemporary Art, 1997.

Goldstein, Ann. *A Minimal Future?: Art as Object, 1958–1968*. Los Angeles: Museum of Contemporary Art, 2004.

Goossen, E.C. *The Art of the Real: USA, 1948–1968*. New York: Museum of Modern Art, 1968.

Green, Samuel Adams. *American Painting: The 1960s*.

Athens: Georgia Museum of Art, University of Georgia, 1969.
Institute of Contemporary Art, Boston. *The Reductive Object: A Survey of the Minimalist Aesthetic in the 1960's*. Boston: Institute of Contemporary Art, 1979.
Institute of Contemporary Art, University of Pennsylvania. *Painting, Drawing, and Sculpture of the '60s and '70s from the Dorothy and Herbert Vogel Collection*. Philadelphia: Institute of Contemporary Art, University of Pennsylvania, 1975.
Ithaca College Museum of Art. *Selected N.Y.C. Artists 1967*. Ithaca, NY: Ithaca College Museum of Art, 1967.
Judd, Donald. *Donald Judd: Complete Writings, 1959–1975*. Halifax: Press of the Nova Scotia College of Art and Design, 2005.
Kertess, Klaus. *Seen, Written: Selected Essays*. New York: Gregory R. Miller & Co., 2010.
Marano, Lizbeth. *Parasol and Simca: Two Presses/Two Processes*. Lewisburg, PA: Center Gallery, Bucknell University, 1984.
Marian Locks Gallery. *The Purist Image*. Philadelphia: Marian Locks Gallery, 1986.
Mary Boone Gallery. *Ralph Humphrey: 1990*. New York: Mary Boone Gallery, 1990.
Mary Boone Gallery. *Ralph Humphrey: Frame Paintings, 1964 to 1965*. New York: Mary Boone Gallery, 1990.
Miami University Art Museum. *A Seventies Selection: An Exhibition of Works from the Collection of the Whitney Museum of American Art*. Oxford, OH: Miami University Art Museum, 1981.
Nordland, Gerald. *Fourteen Abstract Painters*. Los Angeles: Frederick S. Wight Art Gallery, University of California, Los Angeles, 1975.
Philadelphia Museum of Art. *The Pure and Clear: American Innovations*. Philadelphia: Philadelphia Museum of Art, 1968.
Phillips, Lisa. *Painting in Relief*. New York: Whitney Museum of American Art, 1980.
Pincus-Witten, Robert. *Postminimalism*. Ridgefield, CT: Aldrich Museum of Contemporary Art, 1982.
Prokopoff, Stephen S. *A Romantic Minimalism*. Philadelphia: Institute of Contemporary Art, University of Pennsylvania, 1967.
P.S. 1 Contemporary Art Center. *Abstract Painting: 1960–1969*. Queens: P.S. 1 Contemporary Art Center, 1983.
Renaissance Society of the University of Chicago. *Ideas on Paper, 1970–1976*. Chicago: Renaissance Society of the University of Chicago, 1976.
Renaissance Society of the University of Chicago. *The Meditative Surface*. Chicago: Renaissance Society of the University of Chicago, 1984.
Robins, Corinne. *Planar Painting: Constructs, 1975–1980*. New York: Alternative Museum, 1980.
Santa Barbara Museum of Art. *Spray*. Santa Barbara, CA: Santa Barbara Museum of Art, 1971.
Sarah Lawrence College Art Gallery. *'75, '76, '77: Painting, Part I*. Bronxville, NY: Sarah Lawrence College Art Gallery, 1977.
Scala, Joseph A. *Current/New York: Recent Works in Relief*. Syracuse, NY: Joe and Emily Lowe Art Gallery, Syracuse University, 1980.
Siegel, Katy. *High Times, Hard Times: New York Painting, 1967–1975*. New York: Independent Curators International, 2006.
Solomon R. Guggenheim Museum. *American Abstract Expressionists and Imagists*. New York: Solomon R. Guggenheim Museum, 1961.
Sydney and Frances Lewis Foundation. *Late Twentieth Century Art from the Sydney and Frances Lewis Foundation*. Richmond, VA: Sydney and Frances Lewis Foundation, 1978.
Tannenbaum, Judith. *3 Dimensional Painting*. Chicago: Museum of Contemporary Art, 1980.
Tucker, Marcia. *The Structure of Color*. New York: Whitney Museum of American Art, 1971.
University of Michigan Museum of Art. *Works from the Collection of Dorothy and Herbert Vogel*. Ann Arbor: University of Michigan Museum of Art, 1978.
Whitney Museum of American Art. *1969 Annual Exhibition: Contemporary American Painting*. New York: Whitney Museum of American Art, 1969.
Whitney Museum of American Art. *1979 Biennial Exhibition*. New York: Whitney Museum of American Art, 1979.
Wood, Mara-Helen and Ellen Price. *New Work, New York: Newcastle Salutes New York*. Newcastle-upon-Tyne, United Kingdom: Newcastle Polytechnic Gallery, 1983.

PERIODICALS

Aldrich, Larry. "Young Lyrical Painters." *Art in America* 57, no. 6 (1969): 104–113.
Alloway, Lawrence. "Background to Systemic." *Art News* 65, no. 6 (1966): 30–33.
Artner, Alan G. "After Recent Misses, MCA Hits Target with Three New Shows." *Chicago Tribune*, August 10, 1980.

Ashbery, John. "The Perennial Biennial." *New York Magazine* 12, no. 12 (1979): 70–71.
Baker, Amy. "Painterly Edge: A Conversation with Ralph Humphrey." *Artforum* 20, no. 8 (1982): 38–43.
Baker, Kenneth. "Material Feelings." *Art in America* 72, no. 9 (1984): 162–167.
Baker, Kenneth. "New York: Ralph Humphrey." *Artforum* 9, no. 9 (1971): 74.
Baker, Kenneth. "Reviews: Ralph Humphrey." *Artforum* 18, no. 11 (1980): 63.
Battcock, Gregory. "In the Galleries: Ralph Humphrey." *Arts Magazine* 42, no. 4 (1968): 62.
Benedikt, Michael. "New York." *Art International* 11, no. 4 (1967): 64.
Burton, Scott. "A Different Stripe." *Art News* 66, no. 10 (1968): 36–37, 53–56.
Campbell, Lawrence. "Reviews and Previews: Ralph Humphrey." *Art News* 57, no. 10 (1959): 17–18.
Campbell, Lawrence. "Reviews and Previews: Ralph Humphrey." *Art News* 58, no. 10 (1960): 14–15.
Davis, Douglas. "The New Color Painters." *Newsweek* 75, no. 18 (1970): 84–85.
Derfner, Phyllis. "Review of Exhibitions: Ralph Humphrey at John Weber." *Art in America* 64, no. 3 (1976): 106.
Domingo, Willis. "Color Abstractionism: A Survey of Recent American Painting." *Arts Magazine* 45, no. 3 (1970–1971): 34–40.
Dreiss, Joseph. "Arts Reviews: Ralph Humphrey." *Arts Magazine* 49, no. 1 (1974): 57.
Dreiss, Joseph. "Arts Reviews: Ralph Humphrey." *Arts Magazine* 49, no. 8 (1975): 7.
Frank, Elizabeth. "Review of Exhibitions: Ralph Humphrey at Willard." *Art in America* 68, no. 6 (1980): 157.
Frank, Peter. "Review of Exhibitions: Ralph Humphrey at Bykert Uptown." *Art in America* 62, no. 5 (1974): 107–108.
Freed, Eleanor. "A Windfall for Texas." *Art in America* 57, no. 6 (1969): 78–85.
Glueck, Grace. "Ralph Humphrey." *New York Times*, February 15, 1969.
Glueck, Grace. "Whitney Displaying This Year's Acquisitions." *New York Times*, June 10, 1970.
Goldin, Amy. "In the Galleries: Ralph Humphrey." *Arts Magazine* 39, no. 10 (1965): 66.
Halacs, Piri. "Painting to See, to Feel." *Time* 93, no. 22 (1969): 64.
Hamilton, George Heard. "Painting in Contemporary America." *Burlington Magazine* 102, no. 686 (1960): 192–197.
Humphrey, Ralph and Priscilla Colt. "Ralph Humphrey: Statement and Critique." *Arts Magazine* 49, no. 6 (1975): 56–59.
Judd, Donald. "In the Galleries: Ralph Humphrey." *Arts* 34, no. 6 (1960): 54.
Kozloff, Max. "Light as Surface: Ralph Humphrey and Dan Christensen." *Artforum* 6, no. 6 (1968): 26–30.
Kramer, Hilton. "Ralph Humphrey." *New York Times*, January 21, 1967.
Kramer, Hilton. "The Abstract and the Real: From Metaphysics to Visual Facts." *New York Times*, July 21, 1968.
Kurtz, Stephen A. "Reviews and Previews: Ralph Humphrey." *Art News* 68, no. 1 (1969): 20.
Larson, Kay. "Guerilla Tactics." *New York Magazine* 20, no. 5 (1987): 54–55.
Larson, Kay. "Small Talk." *Village Voice*, February 11, 1980: 74.
Levine, Neil A. "Reviews and Previews: Ralph Humphrey." *Art News* 64, no. 4 (1965): 16.
Lippard, Lucy. "The Silent Art." *Art in America* 55, no. 1 (1967): 58–63.
Lubell, Ellen. "Arts Reviews: Ralph Humphrey." *Arts Magazine* 51, no. 8 (1977): 35.
Matthias, Rosemary. "In the Galleries: Ralph Humphrey." *Arts Magazine* 46, no. 8 (1972): 59.
Matthias, Rosemary. "Galleries: Group Show." *Arts Magazine* 47, no. 2 (1972): 68–69.
Mayer, Rosemary. "New York: Group Show." *Arts Magazine* 47, no. 5 (1973): 71–72.
Mellow, James R. "A Summer Show." *New York Times*, May 19, 1973.
Mellow, James R. "New York Letter." *Art International* 12, no. 4 (1968): 63–67.
Mouffarege, Nicolas A. "The Erotic Impulse." *Arts Magazine* 57, no. 3 (1982): 5.
Ostrow, Saul and Shirley Kaneda. "Ralph Humphrey." *Arts Magazine* 64, no. 10 (1990): 78.
Perreault, John. "Too Much of the Same." *Village Voice*, February 22, 1968: 19.
Phillips, Deborah C. "New York Reviews: Ralph Humphrey." *Art News* 81, no. 7 (1982): 161.
Pincus-Witten, Robert. "New York: Ralph Humphrey." *Artforum* 7, no. 8 (1969): 69.
Poirier, Maurice and Jane Necol. "The '60s in Abstract: 13 Statements and an Essay." *Art in America* 71, no. 9 (1983): 122–137.

Preston, Stuart. "Two Esthetic Views: Exhibitions of John Fenton and Ralph Humphrey Are Light Years Apart." *New York Times*, February 6, 1960.
Ratcliff, Carter. "New York Letter." *Art International* 14, no. 6 (1970): 132–144.
Ratcliff, Carter. "Reviews and Previews: Ralph Humphrey." *Art News* 70, no. 3 (1971): 57.
Raynor, Vivien. "Prints of Masters and Others." *New York Times*, July 29, 1983.
Raynor, Vivien. "Ralph Humphrey." *New York Times*, April 16, 1982.
Raynor, Vivien. "Ralph Humphrey." *New York Times*, April 20, 1984.
Rose, Barbara. "It Looks Good on Paper." *New York Magazine* 5, no. 21 (1972): 76–77.
Rose, Barbara. "New York: Group Show." *Artforum* 6, no. 3 (1967): 59–60.
Rosenstein, Harris. "Reviews and Previews: Ralph Humphrey." *Art News* 69, no. 3 (1970): 67.
Rosenstein, Harris. "Reviews and Previews: Ralph Humphrey." *Art News* 71, no. 4 (1971): 53.
Rosenthal, Mark. "The Structured Subject in Contemporary Art: Reflections on Works in Twentieth Century Galleries." *Philadelphia Museum of Art Bulletin* 79, no. 340 (1983): 6–7.
Russell, John. "Inaugural Show." *New York Times*, January 21, 1977.
Russell, John. "The Zeitgeist Signals Just Downstairs on 73rd St." *New York Times*, November 7, 1980.
Sandler, Irving. "Reviews and Previews: Ralph Humphrey." *Art News* 60, no. 3 (1961): 15–16.
Schjeldahl, Peter. "New York Letter." *Art International* 13, no. 4 (1969): 62–67.
Schwartz, Ellen. "New York Reviews: Ralph Humphrey." *Art News* 76, no. 4 (1977): 126.
Schwartz, Marvin D. "Ralph Humphrey at the Tibor de Nagy Gallery." *Apollo* 71 (April 1960): 81.
Simon, Rita. "In the Galleries: Ralph Humphrey." *Arts Magazine* 43, no. 5 (1969): 58.
Smith, Roberta. "Group Shows Revive the Jaded Art Palate." *New York Times*, June 17, 1988.
Smith, Roberta. "Painting in the Heady Days, After It Was Proclaimed Dead." *New York Times*, February 16, 2007.
Smith, Roberta. "Quieter Times for East Village's Galleries." *New York Times*, February 6, 1987.
Smith, Roberta. "Ralph Humphrey, An Abstract Painter and Teacher." *New York Times*, July 17, 1990.
Smith, Roberta. "Ralph Humphrey: Frame Paintings, 1964 to 1965." *New York Times*, September 28, 1990.
Smith, Roberta. "Reviews: Ralph Humphrey." *Artforum* 13, no. 9 (1975): 73.
Smith, Roberta. "Tempus Fidget." *Village Voice*, April 20, 1982: 89.
Staniszewski, Mary Anne. "New York Reviews: Ralph Humphrey." *Art News* 78, no. 9 (1980): 211–212.
Sussler, Betsy. "Ralph Humphrey." *Bomb* 11 (Winter 1985): 24–27.
Vernet, Gwynne. "Drawing Invitational 1981." *Arts Magazine* 56, no. 6 (1982): 25.
Waldman, Diane. "Reviews and Previews: Ralph Humphrey." *Art News* 65, no. 10 (1967): 15.
Westfall, Stephen. "Arts Reviews: Ralph Humphrey." *Arts Magazine* 59, no. 1 (1984): 40.
Wilson, William S. "Ralph Humphrey." *Arts Magazine* 50, no. 6 (1976): 5.
Wilson, William S. "Ralph Humphrey: An Apology for Painting." *Artforum* 16, no. 3 (1977): 54–59.
Zimmer, William. "Surfacing: Ralph Humphrey." *SoHo Weekly News*, April 23, 1980: 60.
Zucker, Barbara. "Reviews and Previews: Ralph Humphrey." *Art News* 74, no. 4 (1975): 98.

Published on the occasion of the exhibition
Ralph Humphrey at Gary Snyder Gallery,
September 13–October 20, 2012

Edited by Garth Greenan
Copyedited by Michael Lacoy
Designed by Judith Hudson, Biproduct
Photography by Christopher Burke Studio
Printed in the United States by Shapco Printing, Inc.

This exhibition and the accompanying publication would not have been possible without the generous time and support of many individuals. In particular, we would like to thank: Beth Humphrey, Guy Reed, Karen Humphrey, Dan Weinberg, Bill Wilson, John Baker, Nina Nielsen, Bob Feldman, Fredericka Hunter, Christophe de Menil, Tom Papa, Noah Pollack, Irwin and Barbara Weinberg, Robert Cicetti, Jason Silva, and Adam Winner.

Endpapers, pages 54, 58–59: Excerpts from the artist's notebooks, c. 1973–1978.
Page 40: Humphrey in front of his painting *Wentworth* (1964), c. 1982.
Page 62: The artist in his studio on New York's Upper West Side, February 1957. Photograph by Emerick Bronson.
Page 64: The artist and his cousins, c. 1952, at a park near Youngstown, Ohio.
Page 65: (top) Humphrey teaching at Hunter College, c. 1978; (bottom) with his daughter, Beth, c. 1980.

Distributed by
D.A.P./Distributed Art Publishers, Inc.
155 Sixth Avenue, 2nd Floor
New York, NY 10013
Tel: 212 626 1999
Fax: 212 627 9484
www.artbook.com

ISBN: 978-0-9829747-6-6